Thirty Steps to Heaven

Thirty Steps to Heaven

The Ladder of Divine Ascent for All Walks of Life

Vassilios Papavassiliou

Ancient Faith Publishing
◊
Chesterton, Indiana

Thirty Steps to Heaven: *The Ladder of Divine Ascent* for All Walks of Life
Copyright © 2013 by Theodore Christopher Vasilis
All Rights Reserved

All quotations from the *Ladder* are taken from John Climacus, *The Ladder of Divine Ascent*, The Classics of Western Spirituality (New York: Paulist Press, 1982).

Biblical citations (apart from those quoted in the *Ladder*) are from the New King James Version (© 1979, 1980, 1982 by Thomas Nelson, Inc. Used by permission.) Where the numbering of the Psalms diverges between the Septuagint (LXX) and the NKJV, the LXX numbering is given first. Another difference between the LXX and other Old Testaments is the names ascribed to the books. Most notably, the books known as 1 and 2 Samuel and 1 and 2 Kings in the NKJV are known in the LXX as 1 and 2 Kingdoms and 3 and 4 Kingdoms respectively.

Published by:
Ancient Faith Publishing
A Division of Ancient Faith Ministries
P.O. Box 748
Chesterton, IN 46304

ISBN: 978-1-936270-89-7

25 24 23 22 21 20 12 11 10 9 8 7 6

Contents

Acknowledgments 7

Preface 9

Introduction 11

Part I ~ The Break with the World

Step 1 → Renunciation 19

Step 2 → Detachment 26

Step 3 → Exile 30

Part II ~ The Fundamental Virtues

Step 4 → Obedience 35

Step 5 → Repentance 44

Step 6 → Remembrance of Death 52

Step 7 → Mourning 57

Step 8 → Meekness/Loss of Anger 62

Part III ~ The Spiritual Passions

Step 9 → Remembrance of Wrongs/Malice 79

Step 10 → Slander 86

Step 11 → Talkativeness and Silence 94

Step 12 → Falsehood 101

Step 13 → Despondency/Tedium 109

Part IV ⸙ The Physical Passions

Step 14 → Gluttony 117

Step 15 → Lust and Chastity 123

Step 16 → Avarice 134

Step 17 → Poverty 138

Part V ⸙ The Spiritual Passions (Continued)

Step 18 → Insensitivity/Lack of Awareness 145

Step 19 → Sleep, Prayer, and Church 151

Step 20 → Alertness 156

Step 21 → Fear 159

Step 22 → Vainglory 163

Step 23 → Pride 171

Part VI ⸙ The Higher Virtues

Step 24 → Meekness/Simplicity 183

Step 25 → Humility 188

Step 26 → Discernment 197

Part VII ⸙ Union with God

Step 27 → Stillness 211

Step 28 → Prayer 218

Step 29 → Dispassion 232

Step 30 → Faith, Hope, and Love 238

About the Author 249

An Excerpt from *Meditations for Holy Week* 251

Acknowledgments

When Ancient Faith Publishing asked me to write this book, my first thought was to decline. One may be forgiven for thinking it an act of singular presumptuousness for an author who lacks monastic experience to write a layman's guide to a classic work of monastic spirituality. I was well aware of both the popularity and the notoriety of the *Ladder of Divine Ascent*. Many praise it as a "must-read" for all Orthodox Christians, while others reluctantly recommend it with a "spiritual health warning" due to its heavily monastic character.

It became apparent that a layman's guide to the *Ladder* was sorely needed, and the criterion for writing such a book was not necessarily a monastic vocation. With that in mind, I took up the offer, and it proved to be a very edifying experience for me. I am therefore thankful to Ancient Faith Publishing and all those who have encouraged me to undertake this project. I am especially thankful to Katherine Hyde, acquisitions editor at Ancient Faith Publishing, and Kristian Akselberg, who made some very helpful suggestions and helped me track down several excellent patristic sources.

Preface

A Brief Summary and Exhortation

Ascend, my brothers, ascend eagerly. Let your hearts' resolve be to climb. Listen to the voice of the one who says: "Come, let us go up to the mountain of the Lord, to the house of our God" (Isa. 2:3), Who makes our feet to be like the feet of the deer, "Who sets us on the high places, that we may be triumphant on His road" (Hab. 3:19).

Run, I beg you, run with him who said, "Let us hurry until we all arrive at the unity of the faith and of the knowledge of God, at mature manhood, at the measure of the stature of Christ's fullness" (Eph. 4:13). Baptized in the thirtieth year of His earthly age, Christ attained the thirtieth step on the spiritual ladder,[1] for God indeed is love, and to Him be praise, dominion, power. In Him is the cause, past, present, and future, of all that is good forever and ever. Amen.

1 A reference to Luke 2:52: "And Jesus increased in wisdom and stature, and in favor with God and men." St. Cyril of Alexandria explains that while Christ in divinity had no need to "attain" virtue, in humanity He had to develop just like any other human being (5th Homily on Luke, PG 72:136D–137C).

Introduction

God is the life of all free beings. He is the salvation of all, of believers or unbelievers, of the just or the unjust, of the pious or the impious, of those freed from the passions or caught up in them, of monks or those living in the world, of the educated or the illiterate, of the healthy or the sick, of the young or the very old.

The Ladder of Divine Ascent is undoubtedly one of the most influential Christian texts ever written. Its author, St. John, is named after it—St. John Climacus (of the Ladder). He is known also as St. John of Sinai, the mountain in Egypt on which Moses saw God and received the Ten Commandments (see Exodus 3 and 31:18), where John was a monk at the Monastery of St. Catherine.

The earliest record of monastic life on Sinai is from a travel journal written sometime between AD 381 and 384. When John arrived at St. Catherine's Monastery at the age of sixteen, probably in the latter half of the sixth century, the monastic community was already well established. Three forms of monasticism were practiced on Sinai at that time: the communal, or cenobitic, form (a brotherhood living a life of common prayer and worship and shared resources, under the guidance of an abbot); the solitary, or eremitic, form (hermits, or anchorites, living alone in the surrounding desert); and the semi-eremitic form (small monastic communities, or sketes, consisting of a spiritual father and one or two other monks living together near the monastery grounds).

St. John of the Ladder came to experience all three forms of monasticism. Initially he lived the semi-eremitic life and then became an anchorite. During that time as a hermit, he occasionally received visitors—mostly fellow monks—and he soon developed a reputation for holiness and spiritual insight. After forty years as a solitary, he was elected abbot of St. Catherine's Monastery.

It was during his time as abbot of the monastic brotherhood of St. Catherine that John wrote the *Ladder of Divine Ascent*, in response to a request from another abbot for a spiritual manual for monks. The *Ladder* describes in thirty steps the monk's desired progress on the path of spiritual perfection. Soon after writing it, St. John resigned from his position as abbot and returned to solitude until his death, around the middle of the seventh century.

The influence of the *Ladder* soon extended beyond the monastic communities, and it has been read and loved by laypeople for centuries. Even outside of monasteries, where it is read liturgically during the Hours, many Orthodox Christians read the *Ladder* during Lent. Notwithstanding the book's popularity, it is not always easy for normal laypeople to apply its teachings to their own lives—lives very different indeed from that which the Ladder addresses. Therefore, simple commentaries such as this (albeit written by someone far less advanced in the spiritual life than St. John) can be helpful.

While it would be misleading or even dangerous to deny that the *Ladder* was written exclusively for monks, by the same token it would be wrong to conclude from this that others have nothing at all to gain from reading monastic literature. But those who read such books should do so with discernment, particularly with guides or manuals such as the *Ladder*. It can be detrimental for a beginner to attempt the ascetical feats and religious practices and devotions of a seasoned veteran of the spiritual arena. But there is gold in the *Ladder* for all of us, if we have the diligence to seek it out and the maturity to sift through those things that are clearly not meant for us.

The pages that follow contain passages from the *Ladder* (in bold type) that I believe are applicable to all Christians, while certain steps of the Ladder that refer to monastic life are examined in a broader context. This is of particular importance when considering the first three steps: renunciation, detachment, and exile. For the author of the *Ladder* is speaking here in very certain terms: the monk must leave normal society to join a remote monastic community, or even become a hermit, and not look back. For those who are called not to abandon but rather to live within normal society, these steps must be understood in less literal terms.

While it is my intention to make the *Ladder* accessible to the average layman, I have tried to avoid the temptation to simply ignore difficult and even questionable passages that may be a stumbling block for believers. Such passages may be the reason many are discouraged from reading it. While this book can certainly be read independently of and without reference to the *Ladder* itself, *Thirty Steps to Heaven* is not a substitute for the *Ladder,* but a companion to it.

Another aspect of the *Ladder of Divine Ascent* worth considering is the very image of a ladder, of a climb and upward journey. Our spiritual journey requires patience and dogged persistence—taking one step at a time. **Many have been speedily forgiven their sins. But no one has rapidly acquired dispassion, for this requires much time and longing, and God.** No one can **climb the entire ladder in a single stride.** Nor do the steps of the ladder necessarily come in the same order for all people. One person struggles with a certain passion that another easily masters; yet the latter struggles far more with a different passion that the former easily overcomes. In other words, what is step ten for one person could be step twenty for another, and any given step may take many years to master.

We must not be impatient or hasty, for the climb is perilous. **There is always a danger in seeking what is beyond our immediate reach.** The famous icon of the Ladder of Divine Ascent clearly illustrates this—depicting monks falling from the heights into the abyss. Complacency and self-certainty are the most dangerous delusions we encounter in the spiritual life, and they are particularly acute for the most devout Christians. We would also do well to remember that spiritual perfection cannot be attained even by the saints. For **dispassion is an uncompleted perfection of the perfect,** while the last step of the Ladder, which is love, is an eternal step that we will never reach the end of, neither in this life nor in the world to come:

> **Love has no boundary, and both in the present and in the future age we will never cease to progress in it, as we add light to light.**

If the spiritual battle seems hopeless and the struggle too much for you, do not be disheartened and do not give up. Our progress in virtue can often seem less like a ladder of ascent and more like a game of chutes and ladders. It would be wrong and a misunderstanding of St. John's teaching to think that those who fail to reach the heights of spiritual perfection in this life are doomed: **Not everyone can achieve dispassion. But all can be saved and can be reconciled to God.** Falling and getting up again, starting over—this is what repentance and Christian devotion are all about.

One final word of warning: Very few people indeed will have climbed all thirty steps of the Ladder of Divine Ascent. If you think you have, you probably need to go back to the beginning.

Part I

The Break with the World

Step 1

Renunciation

A friend of God is the one who lives in communion with all that is natural and free from sin and who does not neglect to do what good he can. The self-controlled man strives with all his might amidst the trials, the snares, and the noise of the world, to be like someone who rises above them.

Every Christian is called to a life of renunciation: "If anyone desires to come after Me, let him deny himself, and take up his cross and follow Me. For whoever desires to save his life will lose it, but whoever loses his life for My sake will save it" (Luke 9:23–24).

Before baptism, we "renounce Satan, and all his works, and all his angels, and all his worship, and all his solemn rites."

Christ tells us, "My kingdom is not of this world. If My kingdom were of this world, My servants would fight . . . but now My kingdom is not from here" (John 18:36). Therefore, those who follow Him are not of the world either: "If you were of the world, the world would love its own. Yet because you are not of the world, but I chose you out of the world, therefore the world hates you" (John 15:19).

St. Paul warns us, "Do not be conformed to the pattern of this world" (Rom. 12:2).

It is clear, then, that renunciation is not exclusive to monasticism but is an intrinsic part of being a Christian. While the monastic life involves a physical separation from the world or from people (the Greek word, *cosmos*, has both meanings), most Christians must live within normal society. What's more, it is often a society that is not Christian and may even be openly hostile to Christian belief and practice. Even if we are living in a big city, getting on with our daily lives along with the rest of society, we are called to renounce the world.

In this sense, "the world" means all those things that are opposed to Christ and to our salvation. "The world" in the sense of God's creation is good, and we are all (even those living the monastic life) a part of it. However remote monasteries or hermitages may be, all monastics lie beneath the same sun and moon, breathe the same air, and share the soil and fruits of the earth with all humanity. But just as the monastic rejects the worldly way of life—the pursuit of wealth, vanity, pride, and carnal pleasure—so too every Christian rejects these things, albeit some of them to a lesser extent. Christian marriage, while it involves sexual pleasure, is not unbridled lust and selfish hedonism; and while we all need money to live, we are not to be avaricious or greedy.

There can be no ascetic life, no true spirituality, if we are not willing to break with the world in terms of what we hold dear and what constitutes the center and focus of our lives. St. John mentions three fundamental virtues that form the foundation of the ascetic life and liberate us from slavery to the things of this world:

> **Innocence, abstinence, temperance—these make a fine thrice-firm foundation. Let all infants in Christ begin with these, taking real infants as their example; for among children no evil is found, nothing deceitful, no insatiable greed or gluttony, no flaming lust.**

We are not seeking the impossible. Our quest is not for something unknown. We all began life as perfect and sinless infants. "Of such is the kingdom of God" (Mark 10:14). What we seek is what we once were, something we all know and have tasted: innocence.

When speaking of things such as carnal pleasure, many say, "Where is the sin? It is perfectly natural." But they forget that by *nature* we in fact mean a fallen nature, a nature that has been distorted by sin, by the knowledge of evil. Thus, as we grow up and increase in knowledge, we lose our innocence. God wants us to have a child's heart. Thus St. John tells novices of the monastic life to look to infants as their example. We can take this to apply equally to adult converts or nominal Christians who have only now decided to make a beginning of spiritual life. God wants us, though grown up with adult minds, having knowledge, wisdom, and understanding, to be like children: "Unless you are converted and become as little children, you will by no means enter the kingdom of heaven" (Matt. 18:3).

Christians renounce the world by living for something other than the world. By living thus, we become the light of the world. This was beautifully expressed in the second century in a letter to Diognetus:

> For Christians are not distinguished from the rest of humanity by country, language, or custom . . . while they live in both Greek and barbarian cities, as each one's lot was cast, and follow the local customs in dress and food and other aspects of life, at the same time they demonstrate the remarkable and admittedly unusual character of their own citizenship. They live in their own countries, but only as nonresidents; they participate in everything as citizens, and endure everything as foreigners. Every foreign country is their fatherland, and every fatherland is foreign. They marry like everyone else, and have children, but they do not expose their offspring. They share their food but not their wives. They are in the flesh, but they do not live according to the flesh. They live on earth, but their citizenship is in heaven. They obey the established laws; indeed in their private lives they transcend the laws. They love everyone, and by everyone they are persecuted . . . yet those who hate them are unable to give a reason for their hostility.
>
> In a word, what the soul is to the body, Christians are to the world. The soul is dispersed through all the members of the body, and Christians throughout the cities of the world. The soul dwells in the body, but is not of the body; likewise Christians dwell in the world, but are not of the world. The

soul, which is invisible, is confined in the body, which is visible; in the same way, Christians are recognized as being in the world, and yet their religion remains invisible.[2]

It is clear, then, that renouncing the world means far more than abandoning urban society for a monastic community. This is part and parcel of monastic life, but not of all Christian life. The rest of us have a powerful role to play within society by living a Christ-centered, not a world-centered, life. St. John of the Ladder was keenly aware of this also. When he was asked how those who are married and living amid public cares can aspire to monastic ideals, he answered:

Do whatever good you may. Speak evil of no one. Rob no one. Tell no lie. Despise no one and carry no hate. Do not separate yourself from the church assemblies. Show compassion to the needy. Do not be a cause of scandal to anyone. Stay away from the bed of another, and be satisfied with what your own wives can provide you. If you do all this, you will not be far from the kingdom of heaven.

The outward circumstances of life are not the same for all of us. Whether we are celibate or married, whether we are living in a monastic community or a marital one, whether we are living in a bustling metropolis or a remote village, we are all called to renounce everything for Christ. This does not mean rejecting and abandoning our careers, families, and friends just for the sake of

---

2 *Letter to Diognetus* 5:1–6:4 in Michael W. Holmes, ed., trans., *The Apostolic Fathers: Greek Texts and English Translation, 3rd ed.* (Grand Rapids, MI: Baker Academic, 2007), pp. 701–705.

doing so. Rather, it means that given the choice between all these and Christ, we choose Christ:

> "He who loves father or mother more than Me is not worthy of Me. And he who loves son or daughter more than Me is not worthy of Me. And he who does not take his cross and follow after Me is not worthy of Me." (Matt. 10:37–38)

But let us not forget that, for most of us, it is through these blessings that we learn to love Christ. If the monastery is the arena for the spiritual training (ascesis) of the monk, then the home, the family, the workplace, the busy urban street are the arenas for those in the world. We must choose the way of life that is most conducive to our spiritual progress. As St. John writes:

> **The real servants of Christ, using the help of spiritual fathers and also their own self-understanding, will make every effort to select a place, a way of life, an abode, and the exercises that suit them. Community life is not for everyone, because of gluttonous tendencies, and the solitary life is not for everybody, on account of the tendency to anger. Let each seek out the most appropriate way.**

Do not think monasticism is the only way to holiness. Even outside monastic life, by confronting all of life's temptations and adversities with patience, humility, and love, especially in our dealings with others—family, friends, colleagues, strangers, enemies—it is possible to reach the very summit of virtue.

There are many roads to holiness—and to hell. A path wrong for one will suit another, yet what each is doing is pleasing to God.

As St. Symeon the New Theologian writes, "Provided they live a worthy life, both those who choose to dwell in the midst of noise and hubbub and those who dwell in monasteries, mountains and caves can achieve salvation."[3]

If God has called you to live in the world, then you are the light of the world. Whatever the outward circumstances of your life, however chaotic things may be at times, you can have a little monastery in your heart where you may retreat to find solitude and strength amidst the troubles and temptations of life. Remember, "The kingdom of God is within you" (Luke 17:21).

3 *The Philokalia: The Complete Text*, vol. 4 (London: Faber & Faber, 1995), p. 20.

Step 2

Detachment

Derided, mocked, jeered, you must accept the denial of your will. You must patiently endure opposition, suffer neglect without complaint, put up with violent arrogance. You must be ready for injustice, and not grieve when you are slandered; you must not be angered by contempt and you must show humility when you have been condemned. Happy are those who follow this road and avoid other highways. Theirs is the kingdom of heaven.

I have yet to get beyond step two of the Ladder, if the above passage is any indication. Yet this sums up what it means to fully imitate Christ, and what is a Christian if not an imitator of Christ?

But why does the above passage fall under the category of detachment? In monastic life, detachment naturally follows renunciation. Having abandoned the world, the monk must guard his heart against yearning for what he has forsaken; he must look not back, but forward. Otherwise, grief and regret will overcome his spirit. Eventually he will come to resent his vocation and see it as an imprisonment and a wasted life, because he has not yet let go of his worldly desires.

For others, too, detachment is integral to Christian living. I have heard married men and women complain that they married too young, that they did not have the opportunity to do the things they dreamed of, that they have missed out on something because they had to sacrifice their will and desires for the sake of their children or spouse. If the monk, having vowed to live a life of utter dedication, is not to look back, should not married couples observe the same rule? "No one, having put his hand to the plow, and looking back, is fit for the kingdom of God" (Luke 9:62).

Many people, monastics and laypeople alike, may not realize it, but marriage and monasticism have a good deal in common. Both are lifelong commitments to something apart from ourselves. Both require the same sacrifice of the will. Both are means of mastering the passions and are paths to holiness and salvation. St. John Chrysostom writes:

> You greatly delude yourself and make a grave error, if you think that one thing is demanded from the layman and another from the monk; since the difference between them lies in whether one is married or not, while in everything else they have the same responsibilities. . . . For all must rise to the same height; and what has turned the world upside down is that we think only the monk must live rigorously, while the rest are permitted to live a life of indolence.[4]

---

4 Προς Πιστον Πατερα *(To a faithful father)* 3, 14, PG47, 372–374.

These two blessed ways of life—marriage and monasticism—are equally difficult and equally beneficial if they are lived in Christ and for Christ.

But there is more to detachment than letting go of our need for self-gratification. The passage I began with makes it clear that we must detach ourselves from our ego, our pride. For it is pride that fills us with anger when we are wronged. It is pride that makes us think, "I don't deserve to be treated like this! How dare they speak to me that way!"

Detachment from pride is the imitation of Christ, because if anyone did not deserve to be derided, mocked, jeered, beaten, and put to death, it is Christ. Who are we to think we deserve better than He? Yet our pride makes us think we deserve respect, dignity, comfort. And if we think as the world thinks, we may be right. Wicked people do wicked things and get everything they want, while good people suffer. Where is the justice in that?

But as Christians who have renounced the ways and, indeed, the justice of the world (for Christ's sacrifice was by no means justice, but mercy), we are to compare ourselves not to others, but to Christ alone. This is why so many saints of the Church faced martyrdom with joy, for in that martyrdom they knew they were following Christ crucified and did not give a thought to "What did I do to deserve this?"

If we are persecuted and hated for no good reason, even if

it is not for our faith, it is a blessing in disguise (a very effective disguise, I'll warrant you, but a blessing nonetheless). For in that moment, we have been given an opportunity to imitate Christ to the full, to truly be His disciples.

Step 3

Exile

Exile is a disciplined heart, unheralded wisdom, an unpublicized understanding, a hidden life, masked ideals. It is unseen meditation, the striving to be humble, a wish for poverty, the longing for what is divine. It is an outpouring of love, a denial of vainglory, a depth of silence. . . . Yet for all that it is praiseworthy, it requires discretion, since not every kind of exile is good if taken to extremes.

If we have renounced the world and detached ourselves from worldly ways, then we live on this earth as exiles. "For here we have no continuing city, but we seek the one to come" (Heb. 13:14). St. John Chrysostom writes:

> If you are a Christian, no earthly city is yours. Of our City "the Builder and Maker is God." [Heb. 11:10] Though we may gain possession of the whole world, we are withal but strangers and sojourners in it all! We are enrolled in heaven: our citizenship is there![5]

5 Homily 17 on The Statutes, adapted from Philip Schaff, ed., *Nicene and*

Spiritual exile often means that we have very different, sometimes completely opposite, values from the world in which we live. Consider the above passage from the *Ladder* and how against the grain of worldly standards this is. We live in an age where self-promotion, competition, wealth, and fame are considered good. For some, these things constitute the very goal of life. To live as an exile, on the other hand, is to remain **unheralded, unpublicized, hidden, masked, unseen; it is the striving to be humble, a wish for poverty . . . a denial of vainglory.**

Christians are not often exempt from the desire for fame, self-promotion, and worldly glory. A great temptation for us Christians is to use our faith as a pious excuse for satisfying these passions, all the while fooling ourselves into thinking that some higher purpose is what motivates us. So often we want everything we do for the Church, every good deed, every effort we make in Christ's name, to be praised, announced, and publicized. It is so easy to say to oneself, "I am doing it for God," "I must spread the gospel," "I must share my faith," "I must be the light of the world," when our true motive is to satisfy our ego. This is why detachment precedes exile. For only when we have detached ourselves from the things of this world can we sincerely act in God's name, and not in our own, while using "God" or "Church" as a cloak to cover our otherwise naked vanity.

But St. John also warns us that exile **requires discretion, since**

Post-Nicene Fathers, First Series, vol. 9 (Buffalo, NY: Christian Literature Publishing Co., 1889), p. 673.

not every kind of exile is good if taken to extremes. I have heard Christians insist on concealing their gifts and talents for the sake of their humility. We must be careful that we do not bury our talent in the earth (see Matt. 25:14–30) in the name of false modesty. The saints and fathers of the Church were truly humble, yet they did not run away from their responsibilities. They recognized the gifts God had given them and used them for the good of the Church.

It is not pride to acknowledge your gifts and talents, as long as you do not become big-headed and think yourself superior because of them. Again, this is why detachment from worldly values is necessary if we are to practice exile with discernment and avoid extremes. A humble person does not refuse to use his abilities for the good of the Church, nor does he use the Church as an excuse to appease his ego. If you hide the gifts you have been given in order to appear humble, then you are very proud indeed. Wishing to appear humble is the worst form of pride. When we have detached ourselves from our sense of self-importance, then we are free to make use of our talents without fear of sin. Therein lies the freedom of detachment and exile.

Part II

The Fundamental Virtues

Step 4

Obedience

Obedience is unquestioned movement, death freely accepted, a simple life, danger faced without worry, an unprepared defense before God, fearlessness before death, a safe voyage, a sleeper's journey. Obedience is the burial place of the will and the resurrection of lowliness.

The first fundamental virtue of the Ladder is obedience. **As flower comes before every fruit, so exile of body or will precedes all obedience.** But why is obedience a virtue? Many regard it as something for the weak, something that does not become a "real man." The only time it is tolerated is when it is considered a necessity. If soldiers did not obey their commanding officers, the army would be a shambles, and this in turn would threaten national security.

But this is not the obedience of which we speak. The virtue of obedience is rooted not in fearful pragmatism, but in humility. True obedience, like true love, cannot be forced—it must be free. Obedience and humility go hand in hand. They feed and nourish one another. We cannot learn obedience without humility, and we cannot acquire humility without obedience. Together, these two virtues can take us to the very heights of spiritual perfection.

From obedience comes humility. . . . And from humility comes discernment. Take courage from this. For if you are able to do something as basic and simple as to obey, then you are already on your way to learning one of the greatest and highest virtues of all: humility. People may think obedience is for children. They are right! No one is as humble as a little child. Thus no one practices obedience better than infants. Let us remember what we said in chapter one: Children are the greatest example of what God wants us to be.

Learn from the Masters

The obedience of which the *Ladder* speaks is concerned above all else with the relationship between the monk (especially the novice) and the abbot (the spiritual guide and mentor of the monastery). Some may find the unquestioning obedience described by St. John uncomfortable, even unreasonable. Where is the virtue in blind obedience? But we must understand that this relationship is rooted in a profound and absolute trust, in the knowledge that the spiritual guide is a man of great virtue and wisdom.

Any art form we wish to master requires trust in and obedience to the instruction and tutelage of an experienced and skilled teacher. Luke Skywalker could not have mastered the ways of the Force had he not placed himself under obedience to Master

Yoda. Harry Potter could not have defeated Voldemort had he not accepted the guidance of Professor Dumbledore. Frodo Baggins could not have destroyed Sauron had he not heeded Gandalf. But let us not limit ourselves to fictitious parallels. In real life also, all great masters had their mentors. Bruce Lee had Ip Man, Mozart had Haydn, Augustine had St. Ambrose.

But St. John speaks of something deeper than merely obeying. The virtue of obedience is a state of mind, a condition of the heart, and a way of acting that is, as we have said already, rooted in humility. It is **self-mistrust up to one's dying day, in every matter, even the good.** It is to be practiced, and its fruits enjoyed, by all Christians. But to whom are we to be obedient?

Obedience to God

It may seem blindingly obvious, but we are obedient, above all, to God. And this is expressed not only in keeping His commandments, but also in the action of prayer. Only an obedient heart can truly pray, for the end of prayer is not speaking to God, but hearing and heeding what He is saying back to us. Furthermore, only a humble person can really pray, because only when we are humble do we not rely wholly on our own judgments, actions, and capabilities.

One foot is advanced towards service, while the other stays firmly planted in prayer. This is the stance for those learning to engage in spiritual combat. This is the life of obedience: prayer and action. We do not remain idle, expecting God to do everything for us. Rather, we act while entrusting everything to Him and His judgment, seeking His aid and guidance, knowing that we can do no good without Him.

Obedience to Others

In the broader sense of virtue, our obedience is to be extended to all people. We said already that obedience means more than taking orders. An obedient person considers nothing beneath him. Being the companion of humility, obedience is the imitation of Christ, who "became obedient to *the point of* death, even the death of the cross" (Phil. 2:8), and who said, "Take My yoke upon you and learn from Me, for I am gentle and lowly in heart" (Matt. 11:29). To acquire obedience is to follow Christ in the Garden of Gethsemane and to become the servant of all (John 13:1–17):

> **Like Christ our God, gird your loins with the towel of obedience . . . wash the feet of your brethren in a spirit of contrition.**

If our obedience is sincere, it bestows upon us the peace from above. If we practice it ungrudgingly (even if we do not like what we have been asked to do), we will find inner stillness and "the peace of God, which surpasses all understanding" (Phil. 4:7):

> **Practice inward stillness amid the twistings and turbulence of your limbs . . . keep your soul undisturbed while tumult rages about you.**

An obedient heart does not seek to please itself, nor does it yearn to get the upper hand. It is not concerned with winning arguments or coming out looking mightier, cleverer, or in any way better than another:

> **Your tongue longs to jump into argument, but restrain it. . . . Hold back your mind, so busy with its own concerns, so ready to turn to the reckless criticism and condemnation of your brother.**

Thus obedience is not passiveness, but humble action that emanates from calm of soul, peaceful silence, and inward stillness.

Obedience in Marriage

Obedience is part and parcel not only of monastic life, but also of married life. Husband and wife are to be subject to one another out of reverence for Christ (Eph. 5:21). They are not to seek their own will, but must subject themselves to the will of the other, for they are no longer two independent individuals, but one flesh. No marriage can work if the two do not sacrifice their own wills in loving obedience.

In the Mystery (Sacrament) of Orthodox matrimony, husband and wife are a paradigm of the intimate union between Christ (the Bridegroom) and His Bride (the Church). Thus husband and wife are invited to attain perfect love and self-denial through marital union in the name of Christ. This means that marriage—no less than monasticism—is a calling to union with God.

Spiritual Fathers

We have said that anyone who wishes to learn an art must subject himself to the teaching of a master. To master the art of spiritual life, we should subject ourselves to the guidance of a spiritual father. But who should our spiritual father be?

It must be said, first of all, that the spiritual father of all his flock, including the clergy and even the abbots and monks under his jurisdiction, is the local bishop. But spiritual fatherhood is delegated by the bishop not only to monks but also to parish priests. Every Christian who wishes to advance in the spiritual life should have such a spiritual father to guide him. He could be the local parish priest. If not, he should at least be a priest with whom the Christian can easily maintain a close relationship (not someone in a remote monastery we visit once a year and write to now and again).

Our relationship with our spiritual father does not resemble that between a soldier and his commanding officer. We call our spiritual guide a father. This implies mutual love, intimate knowledge of one another, and trust, not an impersonal, formal relationship based on giving and receiving orders. Spiritual fathers should always bear this in mind.

A bad natural father does not let his children grow up and become independent; a bad spiritual father does not allow his spiritual children to develop their own discernment. Spiritual fathers must not infantilize their spiritual children. They are not infants. They are grown men and women, many of them with children, careers, and responsibilities. Daily they must make informed judgments, solve dilemmas, and take a lead in many aspects of their lives without the time for or luxury of deferring to the counsel of a spiritual father. A spiritual father helps his spiritual children to develop their own ability to discern correctly; he does not try to replace their discernment with his own. He lets them think, lets them question him that they may better understand and respect their self-knowledge.

Choose a Spiritual Father in Humility

It is unfortunate that many believe their spiritual father must be a monk, a renowned and holy elder of a monastery (or a disciple of such an elder). We forget that our obedience is far more important than the holiness of the spiritual father. St. John briefly addresses this problem in his chapter on obedience:

> **I once saw an experienced disciple who used to boast in certain quarters about the achievement of his teacher. He imagined that in this way he would win glory for himself from another's harvest. But he only got a bad name for himself, for everyone put this question to him: "How then could a good tree grow such a bad branch?"**

I have known people who go off to monasteries seeking spiritual fathers who are so holy they are reputed to have the gift of foresight, before these people have learned to obey the simple advice of average priests. What will you gain from having a spiritual father who is so far above and beyond what you are capable of understanding and obeying? This is like entering a karate tournament for black belts before you have even learned the basics of karate.

What I am about to say may be frowned upon by some, but I will say it because it is true: The fact that a person is holy does not make him a good spiritual father, much less the right spiritual father for you. In fact, there may be something prideful about seeking out such a spiritual father. For in doing so, we have already rejected outright so many good and wise priests for the simple reason that we think they are not good enough for us. If our relationship of obedience is rooted in pride and arrogance, then it makes no difference how holy our guide is; we have already bypassed humility altogether.

As St. John writes in his chapter on discernment:

> Those who wish to discover the will of God must begin by mortifying their own will. Then having prayed in faith and simplicity, all malice spent, they should turn humbly and in confidence to the fathers or even the brothers and they should accept their counsel, as though from God Himself, even when the counsel goes against the grain, even when the advice comes from those who do not seem very spiritual. God, after all, is not unjust. He will not lead astray the souls who, trusting and guileless, yield in lowliness to the advice and decision of their neighbor. Even if those consulted are stupid, God immaterially and invisibly speaks through them and anyone who faithfully submits to this norm will be filled with humility. . . . Yet this perfect and easy rule is rejected by many for reasons of pride.

Choose a spiritual father who can help you realize where you are on the Ladder, and who can help you rise from that step to the next—not someone who is experienced in guiding those who are already far above you. No one joins an advanced language class before he has learned the basics. Find a confessor who can sympathize with your weaknesses and identify with your struggles and way of life. This will help you far more than the lofty wisdom of a holy elder who is so beyond you that you cannot obey his counsel.

A good spiritual father does not sit perched at the top of the Ladder, calling down to those below; he descends the Ladder to meet his spiritual children at their level and climbs with them.

Step 5

Repentance

Repentance is the renewal of baptism and is a contract with God for a fresh start in life.

The Greek word for repentance, *metanoia,* means "to have a change of heart or mind," while the Greek word for sin, *hamartia,* means "to miss the mark." Now if sin means missing the mark, then repentance means getting back on target. It is only when we understand repentance in this way that we can comprehend it as an ongoing, positive, and creative process.

Repentance lies at the very heart of Christian life. The preaching of our Lord Himself began with repentance: "Repent, for the kingdom of heaven is at hand" (Matt. 4:17). All orthodox Christians have taught that there is no salvation without it. St. John of the Ladder is no exception:

> **It is impossible for those of us who have fallen into the sink of iniquity ever to be drawn out of it unless we also plumb the depths of the humility shown by the penitent.**

It is clear that repentance, like obedience, is rooted in humility. A proud person cannot repent, for repentance allows no room for ego and conceit. Pride blinds us to our own sins, while we go on hating those very same sins when we see them in others. Humility alone is capable of seeing the truth, of enabling us to see ourselves as we really are.

We are not speaking here of mere modesty. Modesty is to be found in people of all faiths and of none. Humility is different; it sees the truth because it beholds Christ Himself in reverence and awe. When we are humble, we compare ourselves not to others but to God alone, before whom no one can be proud. This is why the saints are so humble. Saints keep repenting because they keep comparing themselves to the infinite holiness of God. The holier we become, the more sinful we feel.

Many people express disapproval at the notion of religious guilt and penitence. They think it unhealthy and masochistic. That is because they forget that guilt is the beginning of repentance, not the end of it. Let us always keep this double character of repentance in mind: on the one hand, it means to grieve and mourn for our sins and shortcomings; on the other, it finds comfort and joy in God's mercy and love. The end of repentance is to behold the face of God and to hear Him say, "Your sins are forgiven"; "Go and sin no more" (Matt. 9:2; John 8:11). "Your faith has saved you. Go in peace" (Luke 7:50). Repentance springs from humility, and humility makes us free. As St. John writes:

Where there is real humility, all bonds are made free.

Repentance is the daughter of hope and the refusal to despair: (The penitent stands guilty—but undisgraced.)

Repentance is not mere contrition, not a life of endless regret for every wrong we commit or for our every imperfection. Rather, it is a war against the passions. In his chapter on repentance, St. John describes in vivid detail the extreme repentance of certain monks. Even St. John considered their practices of penitence to be severe,[6] but he presents them as an example to other monks, as a reminder that even he does not practice repentance as well as he could. But the outcome of their repentance is something we can and should all aim for:

> **They no longer knew what it was for a man to be angry, for grief had done away with their capacity for rage. . . . Did any of them worry about earthly things? Or pass judgment on anyone? Certainly not.**

When we are occupied with our own faults, we do not concern ourselves with the faults of others. **He who weeps for himself will not be wrapped up in the grief, lapse or reproach of someone else.** When we are truly penitent, anger disappears, and all the

6 St. John refers to a monastery known as "the prison," in which the monks practiced self-flagellation. This is by no means typical of Orthodox monasticism. While such practices are generally rejected as contrary to the Orthodox understanding of monastic spirituality, St. John—while not condoning such practices as a norm—clearly regards the severity of "the prison" as an example of uncompromising repentance. It is, then, their zeal rather than their method that St. John is praising. Despite the influence and popularity of the *Ladder*, the practices of "the prison" described by St. John have never become a characteristic feature of monastic life in the Orthodox Church.

silly things we spend so much time worrying about suddenly seem small and insignificant, because our only concern now is our salvation. At the same time, whatever external afflictions have vexed us appear now not unjust, but warranted: **A sign of true repentance is the admission that all our troubles, and more besides, whether visible or not, were richly deserved.**

Repentance truly liberates us. It brings us back to what really matters. All the stresses and strains of life, all the little annoyances, all the unfairness we experience disappear in repentance, setting us free and giving us peace.

Thus repentance is not passive but active. It kindles diligence and courage, and it is the fruit of hope. For repentance has no purpose if we do not have hope that God will accept us no matter what evil we have done, no matter how many times we fall: **Do not be surprised if you fall every day and do not surrender. Stand your ground bravely.** And let us not forget that repentance ends not in guilt, but in thankfulness. We praise and thank the Lord always, because we never forget His love: **A proof of our having been delivered from our failings is the unceasing acknowledgement of our indebtedness.**

St. John describes repentance also as a **critical awareness and a sure watch over oneself. . . . We ought to be on our guard, in case our conscience has stopped troubling us, not so much because of it being clear but because of its being immersed in sin.** It is important to examine ourselves. Lack of guilt could be the result of adjusting to sin and passively accepting our condition. Time for quiet reflection before prayer can help us to recognize where we are going wrong—not only in what we have done, but in what we have failed to do.

Confession

Repentance leads us also to the Sacrament of Confession. Why is confession a sacrament? Because it reconciles us to the Church and, if we have committed grievous sins that prohibit us from participation in the Eucharist, it brings us back into eucharistic communion with our fellow Christians. Sin separates us from God and from one another. The priest in confession represents not only Christ, but also the Church. St. James writes, "Confess *your* trespasses to one another" (James 5:16). But we cannot always trust people in the Church to respond to our sins in a pastoral manner or to keep sensitive matters to themselves. Therefore, it is the priest's role to represent the whole Church, to receive penitents and assure them of Christ's forgiveness.

Confession is also our opportunity to be healed, to unburden our hearts in confession not only before God, but also before our neighbor (the priest). I have known people who committed grievous sins and left them unconfessed for many years. They were contrite, they were penitent, they had repented and confessed their sins to God, but they had not come to terms with what they had done—they had not been healed—and they carried that guilt for so long! We need confession not because God needs to hear it; He knows what we have done. He sees and hears your repentance before you have even gone to confession. *You* need to hear it. You need to say it. I believe God forgives us more swiftly and easily than we forgive ourselves. But we seek not only forgiveness, but healing. If your conscience is burdened, do not put off confession. As St. John writes:

> **A fresh, warm wound is easier to heal than those that are old, neglected, and festering, and that need extensive treatment, surgery, bandaging, and cauterization. Long neglect can render many of them incurable. However, all things are possible with God (Matt. 19:26).**

Act upon Your Contrition

In monastic life, it is not uncommon for the spiritual father to give his monks penances (intensified prayer, increased prostrations, more rigorous or extended fasting). While this is not so common outside of monastic life, it should not be understood in legalistic terms, as a sort of tit-for-tat: if I do this, my sin is forgiven and atoned for. The purpose of this practice is to transform penance into positive action. Penance could consist of extended periods of prayer, more rigorous fasting, increased charity, or maybe something even simpler: washing the dishes instead of letting your spouse do it, for a change. It is said that Elder Amphilochios of Patmos was a great tree-lover, so he often imposed planting a tree as a penance to farmers who came to him for confession.

But what should concern us here is not whether a spiritual father gives penances, but whether we act upon our contrition and make it a force for good. Penitence should not remain idle guilt. Our humbleness and gratefulness for God's forgiveness should make us better Christians. We can all be better: we can give more time and energy to God and neighbor than we usually do. Repentance should help us do that.

Repentance and the Passions

There is another positive aspect of repentance, which is this: repentance does not mean giving up our passions, but mastering them. The passions are absolutely essential to spiritual life. Without passion, we simply do nothing. Sloth, or despondency, is perhaps the only passion that cannot be turned to good, being not so much a passion as the absence of passion. But generally speaking, the passions, if properly directed, can make us saints. As St. John says in his chapter on discernment:

> God neither caused nor created evil and, therefore, those who assert that certain passions come naturally to the soul are quite wrong. What they fail to realize is that we have taken natural attributes of our own and turned them into passions. For instance, the seed which we have for the sake of procreating children is abused by us for the sake of fornication. Nature has provided us with anger as something to be turned against the serpent, but we have used it against our neighbor. We have a natural urge to excel in virtue, but instead we compete in evil. Nature stirs within us a desire for glory, but that glory is of a heavenly kind. It is natural for us to be arrogant—against the demons. Joy is ours by nature, but it should be joy on account of the Lord and for the sake of doing good to our neighbor. Nature has

given us resentment, but that ought to be against the enemies of our souls. We have a natural desire for food, but not surely for profligacy.

From the above passage it is clear that the saints did not give up anger, but directed it toward sin rather than their fellow man. Their hatred was turned on their own transgressions. Their envy was transformed into a burning desire to imitate the saints. And what of their sexual love? This burning passion was turned to God. It would be no exaggeration to say they had fallen head over heels in love with Him:

I have watched impure souls mad for physical love but turning what they know of such love into a reason for penance and transferring that same capacity for love to the Lord. . . . That is why, when talking of the chaste harlot, the Lord does not say, "because she feared," but rather, "because she loved much" she was able to drive out love with love (Luke 7:47).

Thus repentance is not only penitence and contrition, but movement toward goodness, wholeness, forgiveness, and joy. It is not negative, but positive. It looks not down into hell, but up into heaven. Its fruits are hope, diligence, peace, joy, and self-control. It is a **renewal of baptism**, a baptism of tears that washes away our sins and purifies the soul, giving us a clean slate and a fresh start.

Through repentance you have reached the fifth step. You have, in this way, purified the five senses.

Step 6

Remembrance of Death

The remembrance of death . . . produces freedom from daily worries and breeds constant prayer and guarding of the mind, virtues that are the cause and the effect of the thought of death.

Many of us live in a death-denying culture. People do not want to talk about death or even think about it, as though pretending it will never happen can somehow stop its inevitability. While phrases such as "death comes to us all" and "death is a natural part of life" have become clichés, deep down many behave as though death only happened to other people—people they do not know or like or care about. When a loved one dies, even at a ripe old age, the faith of some Christians is shaken. This is because we are so busy driving the remembrance of death from our minds that we actually forget it is a certain and unavoidable fact.

On the one hand, the fear of death is natural, but we must not confuse this natural fear and the survival instinct with an unhealthy terror. As St. John writes:

> **Fear of death is a property of nature due to disobedience, but terror of death is a sign of unrepented sins. . . . Tin has a way of looking like silver but is of course quite different; and for those with discernment, the difference between natural and contranatural fear of death is most obvious. You can clearly single out those who hold the thought of death at the center of their being, for they freely withdraw from everything created and they renounce their will. . . . The Fathers assert that perfect love is sinless. And it seems to me that in the same way a perfect sense of death is free from fear.**

The remembrance of death is closely linked to repentance, which is why it is the step that follows it. All Fathers of the Orthodox Church have taught that repentance is the purpose of our life. Death brings repentance to an end. What follows death is the fulfillment and consummation of our relationship with God here and now. So in Christian spirituality, the remembrance of death is, above all else, the remembrance of the Judgment.

If death is the end of human existence, then what's to fear? Why should anyone be afraid of nonexistence? Eternity is a far more scary thing than death. But it can also be joyful. Many saints longed for death, not because they had no desire to live but because they longed to be with God. Those who believe there is nothing beyond death may long for it simply because they hate life or want the pain to end:

> **Not every desire for death is good . . . the man who does not want to change his ways may, in sheer despair, actually long for death.**

As one of the Christian virtues, the remembrance of death is rooted in the knowledge that beyond death lies eternity. God is eternal, and so our relationship with Him is eternal. But what will this eternal relationship be like? Will it be eternal joy or eternal torment?

If we love God—if our life has been lived for Him—then God is our joy. If we do not want God, then His eternal presence and loving embrace are hell. How can sinners look upon the brilliant radiance and holiness of God? We think that meeting absolute goodness would be wonderful. This is like thinking of coming face-to-face with the sun as being no different from lying on the beach on a hot summer's day. God is absolute goodness, unbounded holiness, unrelenting love. And we have sinned against Him. We have wronged Him time and again. Thus the remembrance of death is a call to repentance, and **remembrance of the judgment is an encouragement to zeal.**

How would you live this day if you knew it was your last? Different people would answer in different ways. I have known people who had a near-death experience. They said it changed their perspective on life, inasmuch as they decided from then on to enjoy every minute. They really missed the point. If this life is all there is, then whatever you do is rendered meaningless by death.

But if there is no such thing as eternal death, if we face two possible eternities—one infinitely blessed, the other infinitely cursed (depending on whether we love God or hate Him)—then how should we live our last day? Surely, we should pray, repent, give our belongings to those who need them, be reconciled with all those who have wronged us, and ask forgiveness of those against whom we have sinned. Ultimately, this is how every Christian is to live every day of his life: we must pray, forgive, be generous, and live a simple life; we should go to church, confess our sins, endure all things with patience and humility, and show love to all.

When we remember death, life is put into perspective. We will not waste our time on things that are not "good and profitable for our souls."[7] This is why St. John writes, **No one who has acquired the remembrance of death will ever be able to sin.** Our worldly desires are mortified when we remember that death is at the door. At the same time, we seek all the more urgently to do good. When people know they have only so long to live, they begin to get their affairs in order: they prepare a will to dispose of their property, and they seek to be reconciled with those they have fallen out with.

The saints lived each day as though it were their last, and so they always sought forgiveness and reconciliation, they gave away their possessions to the poor, and they spurned the pleasures of life. **The thought of death . . . brings with it chastity and activity.**

7 The Divine Liturgy of St. John Chrysostom, Litany of the Precious Gifts.

Thus the remembrance of death does not mean giving up on life, but living life the way we ought to. It pushes us to do good, and it keeps us detached from the things of this world. Thus it liberates us from the shackles of earthly cares:

The man who has died to all things remembers death, but whoever holds some ties with the world will not cease plotting against himself.

None of us knows the time of our death, yet we must always be ready for it. If we live as though we are going to die tomorrow, we will be ready. We will carry out God's commandments every day and will always be prepared for our departure from this world. Then we can hope that, like the Righteous Symeon, we shall meet our death with hope and joy: "Lord, now You are letting Your servant depart in peace" (Luke 2:29).

This, then, is the sixth step. He who has climbed it will never sin. "Remember your last end, and you will never sin" (Ecclus. 7:36).

Step 7

Mourning

The tears that come after baptism are greater than baptism itself, though it may seem rash to say so. Baptism washes off those evils that were previously within us, whereas the sins committed after baptism are washed away by tears. The baptism received by us as children we have all defiled, but we cleanse it anew with our tears.

Repentance and meditation on death lead to mourning. Thus mourning is the step that follows them. But the mourning of which St. John speaks is not the kind we are all accustomed to. The *Ladder* refers to tears and mourning as a divine gift. It is a gift difficult for those who do not possess it to understand, and it is not easy to distinguish between natural tears and divinely given tears. As St. John writes:

> **Many of the Fathers declare that this problem of tears, especially where it concerns beginners, is a very obscure matter and hard to analyze since tears can come about in various ways. Tears come from nature, from God, from suffering good and**

> bad, from vainglory, from licentiousness, from love, from remembrance of death, and from numerous other causes. Having trained ourselves in all these ways by the fear of God, let us acquire the pure and guileless tears that come with the remembrance that we must die. There is nothing false in these, no sop to self-esteem. Rather do they purify us, lead us on in love of God, wash away our sins and drain away our passions.

> A man misses the true beauty of mourning if he can mourn at will, rather than because he genuinely wants to, or, more accurately, because God wishes him to. The ugly tears of vainglory mingle frequently with mourning which is pleasing to God, as we shall discover by experience whenever we find ourselves mourning and yet doing wrong.

Tears are not always a sign of true repentance. Sometimes people cry not because they are penitent, but because they feel sorry for themselves, or because they have been found out. Sometimes we cry because we fear punishment or are ashamed and embarrassed that people have seen through our mask of piety and recognized us for what we really are. We must be mindful of the motives for our contrition. This is why St. John warns even those who have the "gift of tears" to conceal it as best they can, for fear their virtue will become the cause of conceit:

> He who has the gift of spiritual tears will be able to mourn anywhere. But if it is all outward show, there will be no

end to his discussion of places and means. Hidden treasure is more secure than that which is exposed in the marketplace. Ponder this, and apply it to yourself.

When you are recollected do not show off. Withdraw into your heart, and remember that devils fear recollection as thieves fear dogs.

If your soul is still not perfectly pure, then be suspicious of your tears, for wine drawn straight from the presses cannot be trusted.

Those who are truly humble and have attained the gift of mourning are frequently unaware that they have reached this step of the Ladder. It is for this reason that saints never believe they have attained sanctity. Humility is so tricky because humility makes it impossible to think we are making any progress in humility.

Take, for example, the famous story of St. Sisoës. When he lay upon his deathbed, his monks gathered around him and saw that his face shone like the sun. He began speaking, and they asked whom he was speaking to. He replied, "The angels have come for my soul, and I'm asking them to give me more time to repent." The monks said, "But you have no need of repentance, father." St. Sisoës replied, "Honestly, I don't think I've even begun to repent." St. John Climacus describes such unawareness of one's sanctity as **splendid ignorance**, by which we remain impervious to pride:

I have seen mourning in some; in others I have watched mourning for the inability to mourn, for though they have

it they act as if they did not, and through such splendid ignorance they remain inviolate.

Very few Christians ever acquire the gift of tears, but this is not to say the tears we shed for our sins are worthless before God. On the contrary, they are the fruit of sincere repentance and contrition, and God accepts them with mercy and compassion: "The sacrifices of God *are* a broken spirit, a broken and a contrite heart—these, O God, You will not despise" (Ps. 50/51:17).

The virtue of mourning is more than sorrow. St. John describes it as "joyful sorrow." A contradiction in terms though it is, the first fruits of mourning are peace and joy:

The depths of mourning have witnessed comfort, and enlightenment has followed on purity of heart. Enlightenment is something indescribable, an activity that is unknowingly perceived and invisibly seen. Comfort is the balm of a distressed soul, which at the same time both cries and shouts happily, just like a child. Divine help is the renewal of a soul bowed by grief in such a way that painful tears are marvelously transformed into painless ones.

Those who look upon Christian spirituality from the outside can easily misconstrue contrition and asceticism as negative, as a denial of joy. But those who live the spiritual life know that through these things they acquire a joy that no one and nothing can take away from them. Thus our Lord Himself says, "Blessed *are* those who mourn, for they shall be comforted" (Matt. 5:4).

The Three Stages of Mourning

The *Ladder* frequently describes progress in the virtues in three stages: beginning, intermediate, and advanced. In regards to mourning, temperance is the mark of the beginner; loss of anger the mark of the intermediate; compassion the mark of the advanced:

> **Those making some progress in blessed mourning are usually temperate and untalkative. Those who have succeeded in making real progress do not become angry and do not bear grudges. As for the perfect—these are humble, they long for dishonor, they look out for involuntary sufferings, they do not condemn sinners and they are inordinately compassionate.**

The deeper our spiritual mourning, the greater our love. Peace, joy, compassion: these three virtues are both the beginning of blessed mourning and its end.

Step 8

Meekness/ Loss of Anger

Meekness is a permanent condition of the soul which remains unaffected by whether or not it is spoken well of, whether or not it is honored or praised.

We tend to think of meekness as a personality trait. When we hear the word *meek,* we usually think of someone softly spoken, easily pushed around, someone who never raises his voice, maybe even someone who is weak. But meekness is not the same as weakness, nor is it a particular kind of personality; it is a virtue, and, like all virtues, it cannot be judged by externals.

Our Lord described Himself as meek (Matt. 11:29), yet He smashed up the markets outside the temple in Jerusalem (John 2:13–22); He denounced the Pharisees, scribes, and Sadducees as "hypocrites" and a "brood of vipers" and told them they were going to hell (Matt. 23:13–33). He frequently rebuked His apostles and admonished the Israelites for their faithlessness (Luke 9:41). He was no pushover, until He voluntarily gave Himself up to humiliation, violence, and death, even though as God He had the power—and, indeed, the right—to destroy His oppressors on the spot.

As Christians we are called to take up Christ's yoke and imitate His meekness. This does not mean we are called to be doormats. Instead it means we are to endure wrongs humbly and patiently and to let go of our anger, which is the fruit of pride.

Loss of Temper and the Passion of Anger

The passion opposed to the virtue of meekness is anger. St. John astutely notes that there is a difference between the passion of anger and losses of temper. The latter is not always a sin and can sometimes be helpful both to the one who expresses his anger and the one on the receiving end of it. But anger that is concealed, bottled up, and allowed to fester is like a poison that runs through one's entire body, lingering in the veins and darkening the intellect:

> **I have seen people delivered from passion by the very fact that they had flared up and then poured out their long-stored grievance and, in addition, they got from their offender either some reparation or some explanation for what had caused the long-standing grievance. On the other hand, I have seen men who appeared to be displaying stolid patience, but who, in reality, were silently harboring resentment within themselves. These, it seems to me, were much more to be pitied than the men prone to explosions of temper.**

St. John Climacus echoes the words of that other great tutor of monastic life and Christian spirituality, St. John Cassian:

> If we take St. Paul literally, then we are not allowed to cling to our anger for even a day (cf. Eph 4.26). I would like to make a comment, however, that many people are so embittered and furious when they are in a state of anger, that they not only cling to their anger for a day, but drag it on for weeks. I am at a loss for words to explain those who do not even vent their anger in speech but erect a barrier of sullen silence around them and distill the bitter poison of their hearts until it finally destroys them. They could not have understood how important it is to avoid anger, not merely externally, but even in our thoughts, because it darkens our intellect with bitterness and cuts it off from the radiance of spiritual understanding and discernment by depriving it of the indwelling of the Holy Spirit.[8]

Malice thrives in the deceptively meek and silent. We so often judge meekness and patience by externals. I have seen people remain calm in the face of abusiveness, and after I expressed my admiration for their patience, they confessed the boiling rage that was within them—which, in many cases, remained with them for days, weeks, months, or even years to come. St. John Climacus describes similar cases he himself witnessed even in the sketes of a monastery:

8 *On the Eight Vices*, Philokalia I: 71–72. Quoted in John Anthony McGuckin, *The Book of Mystical Chapters: Meditations on the Soul's Ascent from the Desert Fathers and Other Early Christian Contemplatives* (Boston: Shambhala Publications, 2003), pp. 23–24.

Once, while engaged on some task, I happened to be sitting outside a monastery and near the cells of those in solitude. I could overhear them raging alone in their cells and in their bitter fury leaping about like caged partridges, leaping at the face of their offender as if he were actually there. My humble advice to them was to abandon solitary living in case they turned from human beings into devils.

Again, this is reminiscent of St. John Cassian, who warns us that solitude is no remedy for anger:[9]

When we are angry with others we should not seek solitude on the grounds that there, at least, no one will provoke us to anger, and that in solitude the virtue of long-suffering can easily be acquired. Our desire to leave our brethren is because of our pride, and because we do not wish to blame ourselves and ascribe to our own laxity the cause of our unruliness. So long as we assign the causes for our weaknesses to others, we cannot attain perfection in long-suffering.

Self-reform and peace are not achieved through the patience which others show us, but through our own long-suffering towards our neighbor. When we try to escape the struggle for long-suffering by retreating into solitude, those unhealed passions we take there with us are merely hidden, not erased; for unless our passions are first purged, solitude and withdrawal from the world not only foster them but also keep them concealed, no longer allowing us to perceive what passion it is that enslaves us. On the contrary, they impose on us an illusion of virtue and persuade us to

9 While Cassian is speaking here of abandoning a monastic community for a hermitage, his words can apply to all of us when we seek to be alone in order to avoid anger.

> believe that we have achieved long-suffering and humility, because there is no one present to provoke and test us. . . . Our passions grow fiercer when left idle through lack of contact with other people. . . .
>
> We should always bear in mind our own ignorance of the time of our death, keeping ourselves from anger and recognizing that neither self-restraint nor the renunciation of all material things, nor fasting and vigils, are of any benefit if we are found guilty at the last judgment because we are the slaves of anger and hatred.[10]

In a similar vein, St. John Climacus reminds us to be careful not to confuse having no cause to get angry with not suffering from the passion of anger:

> **Let us not forget, my friends, that evil demons sometimes leave us unexpectedly, with the result that we may become careless about these strong passions within us, thinking them to be of no consequence, and become, therefore, incurably ill.**

At the risk of attaching modern ideas or terminology to the Ladder, it seems to me that St. John is warning us against "bottling up" our anger. It is far better to lose one's temper and let it out, rather than to appear forbearing, patient, and humble, all the while fuming with rage inside. Best of all, of course, is neither to lose our temper nor to allow anger to fester:

> **A sign of utter meekness is to have a heart that is peacefully and lovingly disposed toward someone who has been**

10 "On the Eight Vices," *Philokalia, op. cit.*, vol. 1, p. 85.

offensive, and a sure proof of a hot temper is that a man, even when he is alone, should with word and gesture continue to rage and fulminate against some absent person who has given offense. . . . Anger is an indication of concealed hatred, of grievance nursed.

Pride as the Root of Anger

The passion of anger is not merely a tendency to lose one's temper. Rather it is a spiritual disease that is not always apparent. St. John connects anger with pride and conceit, and therefore sees humility as its cure:

Freedom from anger is an endless wish for dishonor, whereas among the vainglorious there is a limitless thirst for praise. Freedom from anger is a triumph over one's nature. It is the ability to be impervious to insults, and comes by hard work and the sweat of one's brow.

How is pride the root of anger? St. John is not speaking of righteous indignation—anger at sin—but of anger that arises from wounded pride. While people's rudeness or nastiness may seem a just cause to be angry, the passion of anger often has nothing to do with being stirred against sin. Even when someone makes a fair and perceptive criticism with the intention of helping us, anger is sometimes roused within us. Sometimes—either inwardly or outwardly—we lash out at our critic because we fail to see the truth that is being pointed out to us, for only when we are humble are we able to see things as they really are. Moreover, we think ourselves superior to our critics, so that even if we do admit the criticism is correct, our reaction is, "Who are *you* to criticize *me*?" The more prideful we are, the more incorrigible we become, for we begin to see ourselves as superior to everyone—though, of course, we are too proud even to admit we see ourselves that way.

Thus St. John regards anger as a complete contradiction to a life of humility and repentance:

> **Nothing is so out of place in a penitent as an unruly spirit, for conversion requires great humility, and anger is an indication of all kinds of presumptuousness.**

Humility remedies anger because it remedies pride. The more true our repentance, the less wounded we are by anger.

The Three Stages of Freedom from Anger

Overcoming anger is by no means easy, and the *Ladder* provides us with three stages of progress on the path of mastering this passion:

> **The first step toward freedom from anger is to keep the lips silent when the heart is stirred; . . .**

If we are able to keep our mouth shut, even when we are upset, we are at least making a beginning of not giving in to anger. Despite what St. John says about bottling up anger being far worse than losing one's temper, it is also worth remembering that letting our anger out can often be very harmful to those around us. If we strive to refrain from acting or speaking in anger for the sake of others, rather than for admiration and praise, then we are acting with good intentions, and we are at least learning to keep anger from dominating one of our faculties: the faculty of speech.

. . . the next, to keep thoughts silent when the soul is upset; . . .

The next step is to silence our thoughts and not just our lips. We must learn not to dwell on an offense or to think bad things of those who have wronged or wounded us. Anger dwelled upon becomes a grudge, a refusal to forgive and forget, a denial of humility. While we may speak well of others, our thoughts can be full of cursing and arrogant condemnation. If those thoughts come from the heart (intentional thoughts that emanate from the sickness of our soul, rather than fleeting thoughts that enter our minds as temptations), they condemn us before God no less than if we uttered those thoughts aloud. When angered, we must learn to let the anger go. As St. Paul writes, "Do not let the sun go down on your wrath" (Eph. 4:26).

. . . the last, to be calm when unclean winds are blowing.

The final step is not to take offense at insults or be grieved by injuries. How few ever truly master anger! But to master anger does not mean to become incapable of it. On this point let us be absolutely clear. Even our Lord became angry when He saw people turning the temple of God into a marketplace, and He became furious with the hypocrisy of the religious elite. If it is indeed true that Christ, in His humanity, is like us in every respect *except sin,* then we cannot say that all anger is sinful. As the psalmist says, "Be angry, and do not sin" (Ps. 4:4).

Of course, we must sometimes be careful when we speak of Jesus as an example, for as God, He had a right to do and say some things no one else has the right to do or say. But this makes the example of profound humility we see in His Passion all the more powerful and relevant to us. For He expressed no anger when He Himself was the victim of sin, although no one but Christ could ever claim to be undeserving of disrespect and suffering. Our ultimate example is the King of Glory abused and crucified in humility and love.

Anger as the Root of Other Passions

While pride is the cause of anger, anger is in turn the root of so many other sins. Those who are experienced in doing battle with the passions are keenly aware of this. From experience they know that anger leads not only to sins of a similar nature, such as hatred, but even to carnal sins, such as lust and gluttony:

> **I have seen angry men push food away out of sheer bitterness. And yet by this kind of unreasonable abstinence they merely added poison to poison. I have seen others who on being offended for some apparently justifiable reason gave themselves over to stuffing themselves, so that from the pit of anger they fell headlong over the precipice of gluttony.**

Anger leads easily to a loss of gratitude and thanksgiving, which in turn leads to an abuse of ourselves and of others, for anger makes us feel entitled to satisfaction and recompense. When anger blinds us, we seek this satisfaction and compensation in natural instincts and desires.

A Prescription for Anger

One thing St. John recommends as an aid to overcoming anger is singing:

> **Singing, in moderation, can occasionally ease bad temper. But if it is untimely and immoderate, it may open the path to pleasure.**

It is not clear whether he is speaking of singing in general or of chanting (psalms and hymns). Given that he warns against excess and the possibility of immoderate singing leading to another sort of passion, I am inclined to think he is speaking of song in general. Singing, or even listening to music, can help to soothe anger.

But this can be likened to a painkiller that soothes the pain but does not cure it. Just as pills and medicines must be taken in moderation or at the right times, so too must spiritual medicine. But surely the best kind of singing for healing the passions is the singing of "psalms and hymns and spiritual songs, singing and making melody in your heart to the Lord" (Eph. 5:19). For these are not mere songs but prayers.

Such songs can be penitential or praises of thanksgiving. We should begin with hymns we are familiar with from church, such as Psalm 140/141, which we chant at every Vespers service

("Lord, I cry out to You"), or the Great Doxology that we chant at every Matins service ("Glory to God in the highest"). It is far harder to cling to anger when we are singing to God. It can often be difficult to focus on prayer when we are afflicted by anger, but chanting (even when it is with only our mind) makes it easier to expel bad thoughts.

Admonishing Others Without Anger

I said before that anger is not always a bad thing, and there are cases when it is necessary to admonish others. Parents and teachers especially must often raise their voices or rebuke their children or pupils in order to help them understand right from wrong. Even clergy must sometimes do the same. But it is absolutely essential that these actions not be fueled by the passion of anger. This is why it is so important for spiritual fathers to be masters of their passions, for otherwise their attempts to cure others of their spiritual ills end up only adding fuel to the fire of sin:

> **You wish, or rather, have decided, to remove a splinter from someone? Very well, but do not go after it with a stick instead of a lancet for you will only drive it deeper. Rough speech and harsh gestures are the stick, while even-tempered instruction and patient reprimand are the lancet. "Reprove, rebuke, exhort," says the Apostle (2 Tim. 4:2), not "batter."[11]**

11 A problematic passage in the *Ladder* which seems to contradict this is St. John's advice to any solitary who suffers from anger to join a monastic community. He writes, *He will be spiritually stretched and beaten by the insults, injuries, and rebuffs of the brothers. He may even be physically beaten,*

Likewise, St. John Chrysostom writes:

> No matter how just your words may be, when you speak with anger, you ruin everything. This is true no matter how boldly you speak or how fairly you admonish. . . . The Holy Spirit does not dwell where anger is and cursed is the wrathful. Nothing wholesome can proceed from where anger issued forth.[12]

St. Macarius the Great said something similar: "If you rebuke someone and do it with anger, you have allowed a passion to control you. You have not saved anyone and have destroyed yourself."[13]

Patience as the Remedy of Anger

The only way to exercise discipline effectively without anger is by mastering patience. Thus St. John of the Ladder goes on to speak of this great virtue. He describes it in three stages, similar to the three stages of freedom from anger that we examined earlier:

---

trampled on, and kicked, so that he may wash out the filth still lying in the sentient part of his soul. Is this not a contradiction, not only to what St. John says about admonishing with moderation, but even to Christian life in general? How can one justify insult and injury in the name of humility and love? Certainly, we cannot take this kind of behavior as any sort of general standard for Christian living. But it must be understood that those who act in this way must be only those who are so advanced in spiritual life that they can carry out this peculiar type of "edification" with sincere love and discernment.

12 Homily on Acts of the Apostles, 17. Quoted in Thomas C. Oden and Cindy Crosby, *Ancient Christian Devotional: A Lectionary Cycle* (Downer's Grove, IL: InterVarsity Press, 2007), p. 121.

13 *Saint Macarius the Spiritbearer: Coptic Texts Relating to Saint Macarius the Great* (Crestwood, NY: SVS Press, 2004), p. 64.

The first stage of blessed patience is to accept dishonor with bitterness and anguish of soul.

This is almost identical to the first stage of freedom from anger. While we have yet to learn not to be troubled and angered by the words and actions of others, we are at least to learn to endure dishonor rather than lash out and revolt.

The intermediate stage is to be free from pain amid all such things.

This is reminiscent of the third stage of freedom from anger—to be untroubled by dishonor. The *Ladder* does not give us an equivalent to the second stage of freedom from anger, but the third stage of patience is even higher than the third stage of freedom from anger:

The perfect stage, if that is attainable, is to think of dishonor as praise.

Imagine how life-changing it would be to rejoice in what others think of as causes for sorrow and anger! To find joy in what is otherwise a cause of so much sin and misery! The holiest of people, even the saints, are not those who are loved and honored by everyone. Even these blessed people have enemies; even these are hated. To be holy is to transform our response to that hatred into love and joy. If all were saints, we would be living in a perfect world, for it would be a world in which sorrow is joy, in which absolutely everything, however bad, is a cause of thanksgiving and gladness.

Humility as the Remedy of Anger

We already mentioned how pride is the cause of anger and how anger is the cause of so many other sins and passions. St. John brings us back to this toward the end of his chapter on meekness and anger. He personifies anger in the form of a dialogue. Anger, being interrogated about his causes and his enemies, responds:

> **"I come from many sources and I have more than one father. My mothers are Vainglory, Avarice, Greed. And Lust too. My father is named Conceit. My daughters have the names Remembrance of Wrongs, Hate, Hostility, and Self-justification. The enemies who have imprisoned me are the opposite virtues—Freedom from Anger and Lowliness, while Humility lays a trap for me. As for Humility, ask in due time who it is that bore her."**

Part III

The Spiritual Passions

Step 9

Remembrance of Wrongs/ Malice

Remembrance of wrongs comes as the final point of anger. It is a keeper of sins. It hates a just way of life. It is the ruin of virtues, the poison of the soul, a worm in the mind. It is the shame of prayer, a cutting off of supplication, a turning away from love, a nail piercing the soul. It is a pleasureless feeling cherished in the sweetness of bitterness. It is a never-ending sin, an unsleeping wrong, rancor by the hour. A dark and loathsome passion, it comes to be but has no offspring, so that one need not say much about it.

There is nothing more destructive to spiritual life than the remembrance of wrongs. It is, in fact, a complete contradiction to the imitation of God: "If you, LORD, kept a record of sins, O Lord, who could stand?" (Ps. 129/130:3). It is the exact opposite of forgiveness. In the Lord's Prayer, we ask, "Forgive us our debts [Gr. *opheilemata*] as we forgive our debtors" (Matt. 6:12). When a debt is cleared, it is erased, as though it never existed. This is how God forgives us. He tore up the record of our sins on the Cross. They were drowned in the water of baptism, and they are washed away in the tears of repentance. If we refuse to forget wrongs, then we have not forgiven as God forgives—we are still "keeping a record" of sins. Our Lord says, "For with what judgment you judge, you will be judged; and with the measure you use, it will be measured back to you" (Matt. 7:2). It is clear, then, that if we go on marking iniquities, God will mark ours too.

The remembrance of wrongs is the fruit of unhealed anger. When we have mastered and purified our anger, wrongs will be forgotten:

> **The man who has put a stop to anger has also wiped out remembrance of wrongs, since offspring can only come from a living parent.**

St. John tells us: **Let your malice and your spite be turned against the devils.** We are to redirect our anger against sin and evil, above all against our own sins and spiritual failings. To quote a well-known rock song, "I want my anger to be healthy . . . I want my anger just for me."

As a remedy to malice or remembrance of wrongs, St. John recommends a particular prayer:

> **Let the prayer of Jesus put it to shame, that prayer which cannot be uttered in the company of malice.**

It is not clear whether by "the prayer of Jesus" St. John is speaking of the Jesus Prayer ("Lord, Jesus Christ, Son of God, have mercy on me, a sinner") or the Lord's Prayer (the Our Father). Given what I said earlier about the Lord's Prayer and forgiveness of debts, I am inclined to think it is the latter. When we say this prayer, we should pause and reflect when we reach this point, "Forgive us our debts as we forgive our debtors." Here we have an opportunity to put prayer into practice, to consider what this really implies, and to make sure we truly mean what we are saying.

When the wrongs committed against us are great or, if we are not particularly forgiving people, even when they are small, it is not always easy to forgive. St. John advises us to take a small, easy step to begin with:

> **If after great effort you still fail to root out this thorn, go to your enemy and apologize, if only with empty words whose insincerity may shame you. Then as conscience, like a fire, comes to give you pain, you may find that a sincere love of your enemy may come to life.**

In other words, even if we have not forgiven with our heart, we should at least humble ourselves and be the first to say sorry. Then, realizing our own hypocrisy, we may be moved to strive all the more to make the forgiveness sincere. Elsewhere, St. John reminds us that even speaking of forgiveness and insisting on its importance should make us all the more ardently desire to heed our own advice and to practice what we preach:

> **I have seen malicious people recommending forgiveness to others and then, shamed by their own words, they managed to rid themselves of this vice.**

Unfortunately, not only do many of us refuse to take this initial step; if we do, we do not then consider the importance of at least trying to turn this lie into truth. Instead, we remain content with our own hypocrisy and empty apologies, and try to justify our bitter refusal to forgive and forget.

True forgiveness is rooted in the Christian principle of loving our neighbor as ourselves. How do we love ourselves? Different people may answer in different ways. We may not like ourselves very much. Some spoil themselves; others are hard on themselves. Some think of themselves as good, respectable people, while others think of themselves as worthless. But everyone wants the best for himself, everyone wants to be loved, everyone needs compassion and mercy. This is why St. John tells us that feeling pain for the misfortunes of others as though they were our own is a sign of true forgiveness:

> **A true sign of having completely mastered this putrefaction will come not when you pray for the man who offended you, not when you give him presents, not when you invite him to share a meal with you, but only when, on hearing of some catastrophe that has afflicted him in**

body or soul, you suffer and you lament for him as if for yourself.

The greatest cure for the sickness that is the remembrance of wrongs is the remembrance of what Christ endured for sinners, ourselves included:

The remembrance of what Jesus suffered is a cure for remembrance of wrongs, shaming it powerfully with His patient endurance.

When we contemplate God—the only Good One, the only Holy One, the Almighty who created all things—suffering on the Cross in love and humility and saying, "Father, forgive them, for they do not know what they do" (Luke 23:34), how can we continue to bear a grudge? But all too often, we seek to justify our anger. I have often heard people say, "But *this* person knows what he does!" Do you think that would have made any difference? If the Pharisees, many of whom did know better, had repented and asked Christ to forgive them from the foot of the Cross, would our Lord have refused?

Devout Christians will often use the Scriptures, the Church Fathers, and examples from the lives of the saints to make their unhealed passion appear to be righteousness: **Malice is an exponent of Scripture which twists the words of the Spirit to suit itself.** Such self-justification puts an end to repentance and makes all the passions incurable. God's forgiveness knows no bounds, and so, if we truly want to be worthy of the name "Christian," we must strive to forgive with that same boundless forgiveness, to forgive not "up to seven times, but up to seventy times seven" (Matt. 18:22).[14]

Forgiveness is both the response to God's love and, at the same time, the ultimate precondition for receiving God's forgiveness for our own sins: "If you do not forgive men their trespasses, neither will your Father forgive your trespasses" (Matt. 6:15). Thus forgiveness is both the beginning of repentance and its end:

> **Forgive quickly and you will be abundantly forgiven. To forget wrongs is to prove oneself truly repentant.**

The remembrance of wrongs is not a minor imperfection, however natural being permanently angry with those who have done us ill may seem to be. Furthermore, being a spiritual sin (and, therefore, a sin easy to disguise and ignore), the refusal to forgive is no less common in religious people than in anyone else:

> **Never imagine that this dark vice is a passion of no importance, for it often reaches out even to spiritual men.**

Even the most devout Christians can be brutally unforgiving. For though we may know the Gospel like the back of our hand, we yet manage "to make excuses in sins" (Ps. 140/141:4 OSB), even to the point of applying wishful hermeneutics to the Scriptures in order to justify our own weakness. Forgiveness is something the

14 Even this passage is sometimes cited to justify a refusal to forgive by reading "seventy times seven" literally, rather than as a figure of speech meaning "infinitely."

majority of Christians struggle with, whether they care to admit it or not.

But while we must always be compassionate to human weakness and not condemn Christians for being nothing more than human, we should at the very least learn to ask God to help us and have pity on us for being unforgiving. That would be a start! Alas, too many of us refuse to even admit that we *should* forgive, and we fail to see how hypocritical we are for not doing so. Thus we turn Christ's commandment to forgive into a naïve platitude, rather than a very real and stern commandment by which we shall all be judged. Let us pray thus: *Lord, I believe I should forgive; help me to really believe it* (see Mark 9:24).

Step 10

Slander

Slander is the child of hatred and remembrance of wrongs . . . a subtle and yet crass disease, a leech in hiding and escaping notice, wasting and draining away the lifeblood of love. It puts on the appearance of love and is the ambassador of an unholy and unclean heart. And it is the ruin of chastity.

Malice and the remembrance of wrongs naturally lead to gossip and slander. How often have I heard Christians, myself included, go on for years criticizing before others what someone once said or did, without any consideration that the object of their slander or derision has long since repented and been forgiven by God. What a shameful sin this is! God, who alone has authority to forgive sins, who alone is without sin, does not hold the sins of the penitent against them, yet we sinners refuse to forgive. Thus St. John writes: **To pass judgment on another is to usurp shamelessly a prerogative of God, and to condemn is to ruin one's soul.** No doubt St. John had in mind the words of St. Paul: "Who are you to judge another's servant? To his own master he stands or falls" (Rom. 14:4).

To pass judgment is to **usurp shamelessly a prerogative of God** because only someone without sin has any right to pass judgment. Thus with these simple words the Lord shamed those who were ready to stone an adulteress: "He who is without sin among you, let him throw a stone at her first" (John 8:7). Note that He did not say, "he who has never committed adultery," but "he who is without sin." There may be sins we have not committed, and we get on our moral high horse and condemn others because they commit a specific kind of sin that we have not.

We Christians are often guilty of this sort of discrimination. We may say, "I am a sinner," but often what we really mean is, "I am a sinner, but not like *that* person!" "I am a sinner, but I don't commit *that* sin!" We accept "normal" sins and are only outraged by "abnormal" sins. And by what right, and on what basis, have we decided that one person's weakness is more worthy of condemnation than our own? And for what reason do we consider spiritual sins such as pride, hypocrisy, hatred, and slander less grievous than "physical" sins? A chaste virgin can be more defiled in God's eyes than an adulteress or a prostitute:

> **There are girls who flaunt their shamelessness, but there are others who are much worse, for they put on the appearance of great modesty while secretly engaging in abominable behavior. So it is with shameful vices. And indeed there are numerous insincere maidens: hypocrisy, cunning, melancholy, brooding over past injuries, secret contempt for others. They put on a show of doing one thing—then act otherwise.**

There is another reason that to pass judgment is to **usurp shamelessly a prerogative of God**: God alone knows the secrets of the heart. "I am He who searches the minds and hearts" (Rev. 2:23). We see someone sinning and think we have seen the whole person, when in fact we have only caught a glimpse of him at his worst or at his weakest. We do not know whether that person has then shed tears in prayer and begged God for forgiveness. Unfortunately, we are keen to note people's visible iniquities, but we are not so quick to consider their unseen repentance. **Do not condemn. Not even if your very eyes are seeing something, for they may be deceived.** St. John gives us an example from his own personal experience:

> I knew a man who sinned openly but repented in secret. I denounced him for being lecherous but he was chaste in the eyes of God, having propitiated Him by a genuine conversion.

> If a man commits a sin before you at the hour of his death, pass no judgment, because the judgment of God is hidden from men. It has happened that men have sinned greatly in the open but have done greater good deeds in secret, so that those who would disparage them have been fooled. . . . So listen to me, all you accountants of other people's faults, listen well; for if, as is certain, it is true that "you shall be judged with the judgment you have used yourselves" (Matt. 7:2), then whatever sin of body or spirit that we ascribe to our neighbor we will surely fall into ourselves.

Let us note that stern warning: **whatever sin of body or spirit that we ascribe to our neighbor we will surely fall into ourselves.** Again, this reminds us of St. Paul's words: "In whatever you judge another you condemn yourself; for you who judge practice the same things" (Rom. 2:1). And if we have not yet committed the same sins (or, at least we think we haven't), it is possible we will do so in the future. As St. John Cassian once wrote, "A monk is quite certain to fall into the same sins which he condemns in another with merciless and inhuman severity."[15]

Slander is a sin Christians always try to justify. We say, "I am not judging him, I'm just concerned for him." Again St. John of the Ladder gives us an example of such false love:

> **I have rebuked people who were engaged in slander, and, in self-defense, these evildoers claimed to be acting out of love and concern for the victim of their slander. My answer to that was to say: "Then stop that kind of love, or else you will be making a liar out of him who declared, 'I drove away the man who secretly slandered his neighbor' (Ps. 100:5). If, as you insist, you love that man, then do not make a mockery of him, but pray for him in secret, for this is the kind of love that is acceptable to the Lord."**

Slander is also an infectious sin. Many of us find ourselves getting caught up in conversations about others, and not wishing to cause offense, we go along with it. We start contributing our own

15 Conferences, ch. 10, *Nicene and Post-Nicene Fathers*, Second Series (vol. 11), *op. cit.*, p. 419.

judgmental comments. Many Christians are not sure what to do when they find themselves in this situation. It is said that Elder Aimilianos of Simonopetra always walks away when someone begins speaking about someone behind his back. St. John of the Ladder suggests a more confrontational response:

> **Do not allow human respect to get in your way when you hear someone slandering his neighbor. Instead, say this to him: "Brother, stop it! I do worse things every day, so how can I criticize him?" You accomplish two things when you say this. You heal yourself and you heal your neighbor with one bandage.**

By gently pointing out the sin of slander, we not only spare ourselves from engaging in this sin, but we may also succeed in making the slanderer realize his error and bring the whole unpleasant conversation to an abrupt end.

Slander is a sure sign that we are not truly repentant. "If we are on the watch to see our own faults, we shall not see those of our neighbor."[16]

> **Those who pass speedy and harsh judgments on the sins of their neighbors fall into this passion because they themselves have so far failed to achieve a complete and unceasing memory of and concern for their own sins. Anyone untrammeled by self-love and able to see his own faults for what they are would worry about no one else in this life.**

16 Abba Moses, *Seven Instructions*. Quoted in Mary Gerhart and Fabian E. Udoh, *The Christianity Reader* (University of Chicago Press, 2007), p. 252.

Fire and water do not mix, neither can you mix judgment of others with the desire to repent.

I have said before that pride blinds us to the truth. This is never more obvious than in the sin of gossip and slander. For often we consider the minor failings of our neighbor more worthy of anger and derision than our most grievous iniquities. It is not uncommon for someone who has committed sins of hatred, envy, violence, theft, or sexual perversion to condemn another for simply being annoying, for boasting, smoking, or swearing. If we were as outraged by our own sins as we are by the foibles of others, we would all be saved. We condemn minor faults in others while we overlook our own grievous sins, not out of ignorance, but because we forget God; we think if we conceal our sins from one another, the sin is of no consequence:

I have known men who secretly had committed very grave sins and had not been found out, yet cloaked in their supposed goodness they lashed out against people who had done something minor in public.

Those sins that are visible or audible tend to be the sins that are condemned most, while more serious passions are concealed and go unchecked.

To refrain from judgment is the surest path to forgiveness. There is a famous story about a lazy, sinful, and disobedient monk. As he lay on his deathbed, an angel appeared to him holding a large scroll. When he unfolded it, the monk saw that it was extremely long. The angel said, "This is the record of your sins." The monk replied, "Among all those sins, is there written the sin that I ever judged anyone?" The angel tore up the scroll, and the monk left the world in peace to meet his Maker.

Thus St. John writes:

> **Do not make judgments, and you will travel no quicker road to the forgiveness of your sins. "Judge not, so that you may not be judged" (Luke 6:37).**

And while not judging can be enough to save even the most sinful of people, judging can be enough to condemn the most virtuous:

> **Self-esteem, even when there are no other attendant vices, can bring a man down. Similarly, if we have got into the habit of passing judgments, we can be destroyed completely by this alone, for the Pharisee was condemned for this very thing.**

How easily we seek fault in others, and with what difficulty we look for the good in them! We ought to look for the best in people, and we should never forget that we do not know the hearts of others, nor do we know all the circumstances of their life:

> **A charitable and sensible mind takes careful note of the virtues it observes in another, while the fool goes looking for faults and defects.**

If we can overcome the passion of slander, we will certainly be on the blessed road of love and repentance:

> **This is the ninth step, and he who succeeds in it has practiced love or mourning.**

Step 11

Talkativeness and Silence

> Talkativeness is the throne of vainglory on which it loves to preen itself and show off. Talkativeness is a sign of ignorance, a doorway to slander, a leader of jesting, a servant of lies, the ruin of compunction, a summoner of despondency, a messenger of sleep, a dissipation of recollection, the end of vigilance, the cooling of zeal, the darkening of prayer.
>
> Intelligent silence is the mother of prayer, freedom from bondage, custodian of zeal, a guard on our thoughts . . . a friend of tears, a sure recollection of death . . . a companion of stillness, the opponent of dogmatism, a growth of knowledge, a hand to shape contemplation, hidden progress, the secret journey upward.

Some years ago, I was listening to a priest talking about silence—he was trying to explain to me why it is a virtue. I do not actually recall what he was saying, but I remember being impressed. As he spoke, he glanced up to the clock on the wall. Mid-speech he abruptly ended the monologue, and with his head in his hands he exclaimed, "I can't believe I just spent an hour talking about silence!"

In a similar way, halfway through his chapter on talkativeness, St. John of the Ladder writes, **I would prefer not to write too much about this, despite the urgings of my wily passions.** This is no doubt the reason it is one of the shortest chapters in the *Ladder*. Yet it acts as a sort of appendix to the previous step on slander. He begins:

> **The brief discussion in the previous chapter was concerned with the great danger of passing judgment on others, or rather with being judged and being punished by one's tongue, and it touched on the fact that this vice can lay hold of the most apparently spiritual people.**
>
> **The time has come now to indicate the cause of this vice and to give an adequate account of the door by which it enters—or, more accurately, by which it goes out.**

Silence has always been a practice of monasticism, Christian and non-Christian alike. Why is so much importance attached to silence in all forms of ascetic spirituality? Because the more we speak, the less we listen; the more we hear the sound of our own voice, the more we drown out the silent voice of our conscience. While vows of silence are not a characteristic feature of Eastern Orthodox monasticism, silence has always been considered an important aspect of spiritual life and contemplation. This is inspired by a warning of our Lord: "Every idle word men may speak, they will give account of it in the day of judgment" (Matt. 12:36).

I think we have all experienced the harm one word too many can do. Consider how many times you, or someone you know, has made an off-the-cuff remark or a bad joke that has hurt someone's feelings or poisoned a relationship. Now consider how many times you have spent hours happily chatting to people and then walked away feeling empty inside or overloaded with pointless information, along with a sudden urge for peace and a burning need to just get away and retreat into silence.

A fundamental principle of Christian asceticism and spirituality is that our whole being—every part of us—is to be disciplined, purified, and given to God. This applies also to the tongue. "If anyone does not stumble in word, he *is* a perfect man, able also to bridle the whole body" (James 3:2).

Orthodox spirituality is "wholesome" asceticism. By this I mean our focus is not on a particular sin or faculty. I have known, for example, Christian groups, movements, or projects that focus entirely on one particular sin or passion, be it premarital sex, alcoholism, drug addiction, or abortion. The result is a fanatical obsession with one vice at the cost of all else.

The goal of Orthodoxy is union with God and not merely avoiding sin, much less any one particular sin. It therefore stands to reason that talkativeness, which many may consider a very minor fault, is considered as much a passion and a tool of sin as any other vice. While we may think of talkativeness as a bad quality, very few usually connect it with sin. But as long as we consider the tongue to be autonomous—something that falls outside the scope of Christian ascesis, something independent of God—it will inevitably become a tool of sin. As St. James writes:

> The tongue *is* a fire, a world of iniquity. The tongue is so set among our members that it defiles the whole body, and sets on fire the course of nature; and it is set on fire by hell. . . . No man can tame the tongue. *It is* an unruly evil, full of deadly poison. With it we bless our God and Father, and with it we curse men, who have been made in the similitude of God. Out of the same mouth proceed blessing and cursing. My brethren, these things ought not to be so. (James 3:6, 8–10)

Silence is the fruit of repentance, mourning, and the remembrance of death. Even the chattiest of people are silenced when they are faced with somber and sobering thoughts. When we remember our sins, when we remember death and judgment, we can find no place for idle words. Thus St. John writes:

> **The man who recognizes his sins has taken control of his tongue, while the chatterer has yet to discover himself as he should.**

> **The man who is seriously concerned about death reduces the amount of what he has to say, and the man who has received the gift of spiritual mourning runs from talkativeness as from a fire.**

By contrast, when we are spiritually lazy, we try to fill the vacuum with pointless chattering. The *Ladder* pinpoints three fundamental causes of such talkativeness.

1. A Bad or Relaxed Lifestyle

Words are easy, whereas prayer, hard work, fasting, study, and restraint require recollection, contemplation, thoughtfulness, and action. When these things are lacking, we spend far too much time sitting around talking. And let us not make the mistake of thinking that constantly speaking of spiritual or theological matters always justifies this passion of talkativeness. For incessantly speaking of such matters while not acting upon them is of little benefit to us. As St. Maximus the Confessor aptly wrote, "Theology without works is the theology of demons."[17]

But let us also be careful not to go to extremes. For a good word can bring hope, peace, comfort, enlightenment, and joy. Sometimes our own words can even remind us that we should be trying harder to reach our own ideals, to heed our own advice, to practice the very thing we are preaching. All things must be exercised in moderation. There is "a time to keep silence, and a time to speak" (Eccl. 3:7). One of the many great Mothers of the Church, St. Cassiani, a rather outspoken woman for her day, once said, "I hate silence when it is time to speak!"

2. Vainglory

Vainglory is what prompts us to boast and to speak with the intention of impressing others. It is also what prompts us to lie through our teeth about what we know or what we have done or experienced. From the average Joe in the pub bragging about how much he drank last night or the last fight he got into, to the devout Christian pretending the information he has gleaned from conversations with fellow Christians is the result of real scholarly

17 Letter 20 (PG 91, 601C).

knowledge—we are all guilty of lying or exaggerating in order to make ourselves look better than we really are.

The solution is as simple as it is difficult: humility. For wanting to be seen as greater than we are in the eyes of others is nothing less than vanity, a sign that we have forgotten God, who cannot be fooled by pretense.

3. Gluttony

This may seem a more surprising cause of talkativeness. But the reason for it is fairly straightforward. The more lax we are in disciplining our bodies, the less restrained our words. It is no coincidence that social interaction is almost always accompanied by food and drink. Talking and consumption nearly always go hand in hand. Sometimes this rather natural and innocent combination can become a more serious problem, as is the case with people who find it extremely difficult to socialize if they are not at least slightly inebriated. Such gluttony (drunkenness is not usually considered gluttony, but in reality is a common form of it) is often closely connected to talkativeness. Furthermore, when gluttony leads to inebriation, we often lose complete control of our tongue. Therefore, we must guard ourselves against excess if we wish to keep our tongues disciplined.

It would be a mistake, however, to limit our understanding of talkativeness to the tongue. One can do as much harm with the written word as he can with the spoken word. Nowhere is this more apparent than in our modern forms of digital communication, such as Twitter and Facebook. The aggression and venomous judgmentalism one so often finds in these places, especially on Orthodox discussion forums, is breathtaking. It may be the case that many a "troll" is by nature a quiet person, but put him in front of a screen, and the poison comes spewing forth! But useless online chatter is not always of an aggressive or judgmental nature; sometimes it is a cry for attention. It may be that the cause of constant talking (and that includes incessant tweeting and Facebooking) is a desire for recognition, a need to be noticed and appreciated.

The solution to controlling, or rather, purifying our speech (whether our words are spoken or written) is purifying the heart:

> A good man out of the good treasure of his heart brings forth good; and an evil man out of the evil treasure of his heart brings forth evil. For out of the abundance of the heart his mouth speaks. (Luke 6:45)

The more pure our hearts, the more pure our speech; the more considerate and thoughtful and recollected we are through a life of prayer and contemplation, the less harm our words will cause. Thus only the pure in heart are able to purify the tongue and use it as a tool for good without it leading us time and again into a whole host of troubles.

This is the eleventh step. He who succeeds in taking it has with one blow cut off a host of evils.

Step 12

Falsehood

Various kinds of harm can be observed in the passions, and lying is no exception. So one judgment awaits the man who lies out of fear, another the liar who has nothing at all to worry about. One man lies for the sheer pleasure of it, another for amusement, another to raise a laugh among bystanders, another to trap his brother and do him harm.

In the previous chapter, I said that when the tongue is not submitted to God to be disciplined and purified, it will inevitably become a tool for sin. Our words may become a weapon to hurt our neighbor, by saying cruel things to them or by slandering them. Talking too much may lead us to making a distasteful joke or mocking someone in jest when they are in a fragile frame of mind. Talking too much even on matters of theology can lead us to speaking heresies without thinking. Another obvious sin that is empowered by the gift of speech is falsehood; thus it follows on from the previous chapter on talkativeness.

Laughter

Before I address the subject of falsehood, I would like to touch upon another matter St. John tackles in this brief chapter: joking and laughter.

It is not entirely clear whether he tackles this issue, albeit in just one paragraph, because he considers falsehood and laughter to be intimately connected. If that is the case, there is no explanation as to why. Most likely, in this author's opinion, he sees lying, embellishing, exaggerating, and dramatizing as a way of entertaining others:

> **I have seen men, proud of their ability to lie, and exciting laughter by their clowning and joking, who have miserably destroyed in their hearers the habit of mourning.**

It is a passage that may raise eyebrows for many. It may even seem unreasonable and excessively austere. Laughter here seems to be greatly discouraged as a real obstacle to repentance and spiritual mourning. But for most of us, laughter is a wonderful thing. We have all heard the expression, "Laughter is the best medicine." Surely our lives would be unbearably dull, and our literature considerably poorer, without wit.

So why is St. John so negative about joking and laughter? Perhaps an example I am sure we can all identify with will help. Have you ever heard or seen something so funny you found yourself laughing uncontrollably for minutes, even hours? That can wreak havoc with a monk's prayer. Before he knows it, a day, or maybe two or three have gone by, and the monk has barely managed to say his customary prayers, and if he has, his heart and mind were not really in them since they were distracted by laughter. Thus St. John warns monks: **the jokes will start coming back to you when you are at prayer**. What on earth monks or nuns could see or hear in a monastery that would create such hysterical laughter is quite beyond me, but if St. John addressed the issue, it probably means that he knew it to happen back in his day, and no doubt it still happens today.

But is it reasonable to apply such a humorless discipline to our own lives? I have known people who were in a state of despair and despondency to be lifted out of that dreadful condition by wit and laughter. Like the gift of speech, laughter can be used for good or ill; it can be moderate or excessive; it can be used at the right time or the wrong time. But I am willing to go even further and say that this need for moderation applies even to those living the monastic life.

A wonderful example is a well-known story about St. Anthony. A hunter saw Anthony's monks lounging around and laughing. He was shocked by this and interrogated St. Anthony about this matter. The saint responded to the hunter by telling him to draw an arrow from his quiver and fire it with his bow. He did as the saint asked. St. Anthony then told him to fire another arrow, and the hunter complied. After the saint told him to fire a third, the hunter said, "If I keep stretching my bow, it will break." St. Anthony replied, "It is the same with people. If you place too much strain on them, they will soon break."

Lying

Let us now return to the main theme of Step Twelve of the Ladder: falsehood. This is by no means an easy subject to tackle, because falsehood is a very broad word. It covers a whole range of things, from breaking the ancient commandment, "You shall not bear false witness against your neighbor" (Ex. 20:16), which is, of course, a direct violation of the mother of the commandments, "Love your neighbor as yourself" (Lev. 19:18), to saying, "You look nice" to a woman in a skirt she just bought which you actually think makes her look ridiculous.

As St. John points out toward the end of his brief chapter on falsehood, we cannot put all lies into one category, let alone condemn every lie as a sin. He mentions an example from Scripture (Josh. 2:1) that liars frequently appealed to in order to justify their love of falsehood. (In this passage, the prostitute, Rahab, lies about the whereabouts of Joshua's men in order to protect them.)

A similar case of lying out of necessity is to be found in Genesis 12:11–13, when Abraham tells his wife to say she is his sister, for fear envious men will kill him and take his wife for themselves.

St. John is naturally concerned that people will go on appealing to these passages in order to avoid dealing with the passion of falsehood. At the same time, he does not deny that these

Old Testament saints committed no sin by lying in those cases. Instead, he reminds us that only those who are already completely free of this passion of falsehood are able to lie without sin:

> **Only when we are completely free of the urge to lie may we resort to it, and then only in fear and out of necessity.**

We have said before that God wants us to "become as little children" (Matt. 18:3). The more childlike in heart we become, the less we will lie, for falsehood is completely alien to innocence:

> **A baby does not know how to lie, and neither does a soul cleansed of evil.**

Rumors and Gossip

If it is indeed a grievous sin to bear false witness against our neighbor, is it not also a terrible thing to spread unfounded gossip about our neighbor? Nowhere is the propensity for self-justification more apparent than in the sin of gossip and slander. All the time, I hear Christians spreading malicious rumors about others and justifying it by saying, "I heard this from a reliable source." Two things must be said about this:

1. No doubt this "reliable" source received this information from another "reliable" source, and that "reliable" source found out from another "reliable" source. Before you know it, a malicious rumor has spread and become exaggerated over time through a chain of "reliable" sources. Meanwhile, a person's reputation has been ruined, or others have become secretly

suspicious of him, all because you could not resist a bit of juicy gossip. Spreading malicious rumors about someone is not much better than bearing false witness against him.

2. Reliable or not, founded or not, we should not spread such rumors. Just as we would not like others to expose our sins, mistakes, and stupid off-the-cuff remarks, so too we should not expose the shame of others. Keeping our mouths shut, even if we know for a fact what someone has done, is the easiest expression of love and compassion. Yet how few of us manage even that!

The extremely destructive nature of gossip has been beautifully expressed in the following anecdote:

> There was once a man who loved entertaining people with juicy gossip. Sometimes the rumors he spread were true; other times they were embellished to be more entertaining; still other times they were completely false.
>
> One day, he learned that a man's reputation had been ruined as a result of something he had said in conversation. Wracked with guilt, he went to see his rabbi. He told him what had happened and asked if there was any way he could make amends.
>
> The rabbi asked, "Do you have any feather pillows in your house?"
>
> "Yes," the man replied, "I have many."
>
> "Take one," said the rabbi, "cut it open, and throw the feathers out of the window. Then come and see me tomorrow."
>
> The next day the man went to see the rabbi again and

said, "Rabbi, I did as you asked. What do you want me to do now?"

The rabbi replied, "Go and find every single one of those feathers and put them back into the pillow."

In disbelief, the man replied, "But—but those feathers are long gone. That is impossible! You know that!"

"Indeed," said the rabbi, "and that is how it is with our words when we gossip."

False Promises

Another form of lying is making false oaths. Christ warns us against this in His Sermon on the Mount:

> "Again you have heard that it was said to those of old, 'You shall not swear falsely, but shall perform your oaths to the Lord.' But I say to you, do not swear at all." (Matt. 5:33–34)

This is an extension of the ancient commandment, "You shall not take the name of the LORD your God in vain" (Ex. 20:7). Knowing that promises cannot always be kept for reasons beyond our control, our Lord discourages us from making promises in God's name, thereby making His name unbinding and of no effect. He goes yet further and tells us not to swear by anything at all:

> "Do not swear at all: neither by heaven, for it is God's throne; nor by the earth, for it is His footstool; nor by Jerusalem, for it is the city of the great King. Nor shall you swear by your head, because you cannot make one hair white or black." (Matt. 5:34–36)

So Christ commands us to be not only honest and well-meaning, but simple and straight-talking, not allowing our tongues to utter empty words or promises that may be broken by unforeseen events or due to our limited knowledge:

> "Let your 'Yes' be 'Yes,' and your 'No,' 'No.' For whatever is more than these is from the evil one." (Matt. 5:37)

Hypocrisy

The passion of falsehood is something deeper than telling a lie out of necessity or to avoid causing needless offense. It is rooted in one of the worst sins of all: hypocrisy.

> **Hypocrisy is the mother of lying and frequently its cause. Some would argue that hypocrisy is nothing other than a meditation on falsehood, that it is the inventor of falsehood laced with lies.**

The original meaning of the word *hypocrisy* is "pretense," and *hypocrite* means "actor." For as long as we are pretending to be something we are not, inasmuch as we want others to see us not as we are, but as we want to be seen, we will be an embodiment of falsehood.

The passion of falsehood is a sickness of the heart, not an act of necessity. Thus only when we have purified our hearts can we be liberated from the sin of falsehood.

Step 13

Despondency/Tedium

Tedium is a paralysis of the soul, a slackness of the mind, a neglect of religious exercises, a hostility to vows taken. It is an approval of worldly things. It is a voice claiming that God has no mercy and no love of men. It is a laziness in the singing of psalms, a weakness in prayer, a stubborn urge for service, a dedication to the work of the hands, an indifference to the requirement for obedience.

We said before that the passions are not to be eliminated but redirected. Anger, envy, lust, hatred are not in themselves bad; properly directed and controlled, they can bring us closer to God. The only exception is despondency or tedium. This is the only passion, if it can be called a passion, that cannot be redirected and turned to good, because it is not so much a passion as an absence of passion.

There is a particular virtue available to overcome all the other passions. But tedium is a kind of total death for the monk.

What, exactly, is despondency or tedium? It is not mere laziness. It is not simply a physical passion. It is in fact a spiritual slothfulness and indifference. St. John astutely points out that this kind of laziness comes upon us only in the context of our spiritual life, and it can often take on the appearance of diligence, activity, and busyness:

> **Tedium reminds those at prayer of some job to be done, and in her brutish way she searches out any plausible excuse to drag us from prayer. . . . When the psalms do not have to be sung, tedium does not arise, and the Office is hardly over when the eyes are ready to open again.**

We have all experienced this tedium. When we have to say our prayers or go to church, we think, "I'm tired. I've been working hard all week. I deserve a break." But we are not too tired to go out for a few drinks or engage in some other spiritually unprofitable activity. While people sometimes claim that the Divine Liturgy is too early for them to attend, they have no problem getting up several hours earlier to go to work or to pick up a friend at the airport.

Simply put, tedium is putting spiritual life on the back burner and subjecting it to convenience. We simply do not consider it as important as other things. If I don't get up for work, I'll lose my job. If I don't get up in time to get to the airport, my friend will be left waiting. We do not often apply the same sense of urgency and priority to prayer and worship. Of course, physical tiredness can play a part. It is natural for us sometimes to be so exhausted that we do not have as much time and energy for prayer as we would like. But this is tiredness, not despondency. Despondency is having the time and energy, but not caring enough to dedicate them to spiritual life, though we have plenty of time and energy for entertainment, work, family, or other activities.

In monasticism, this tedium is no less a temptation than for the rest of us. St. John was well aware of the temptation to use the duty of Christians to help the poor and sick as an excuse for tedium. He warns monks not to use charitable work (a fundamental characteristic of Christian life) as a means of shunning prayer:

> **Tedium loves to be involved in hospitality, urges the hermit to undertake manual labor so as to enable him to give alms, and exhorts us to visit the sick, recalling even the words of Him Who said, "I was sick and you came to visit me" (Matt. 25:36).**

What Can We Do?

What is the solution to tedium of spirit? How can we get out of this pit of indifference and spiritual slothfulness? St. John suggests two things: thinking on our sins and thinking of the eternal blessings that await the faithful:

> **The man who mourns for himself does not suffer from tedium. This tyrant should be overcome by the remembrance of past sins, battered by hard manual labor and brought to book by the thought of the blessings to come.**

There are other simple things that can help us: the sight of an icon in the home, the smell of incense, the sound of chanted hymns—these can often snap us out of our tedium. Our senses are truly a gateway to heaven. In every Christian home, icons, incense, and hymns should be present. Every Christian home should be a domestic church, with a special place of prayer (what some Orthodox Christians refer to as a prayer corner) and an icon in every room. We may grow so accustomed to these that we ignore them most of the time. But now and again, they catch our eye and bring our minds back to where they should be.

We should also make time for quiet reflection and the reading of the Scriptures. This can and should instill in us a desire for prayer. It does not even have to take up a great deal of time. One chapter of Scripture a day does not take long at all, but we should read prayerfully and attentively, and meditate on the meaning of what we have read.

St. John often concludes his chapters on the passions by personifying the passions and presenting us with a scene of a passion on trial and under interrogation. The passion in question reveals its causes and effects, showing us the relationship between one passion and another. In the case of tedium, prayer is revealed as its greatest enemy:

> **"I cannot lay my head among those who are truly obedient, and I live quietly where I may. I have many mothers—Stolidity of Soul, Forgetfulness of the Things of Heaven, or, sometimes, Too Heavy a Burden of Troubles. My children**

who live with me are Changing from Place to Place, Disobedience to One's Superior, Forgetfulness of the Judgment to Come, and sometimes, the Abandonment of One's Vocation. The singing of psalms and manual labor are my opponents by whom I am now bound. My enemy is the thought of death, but what really slays me is prayer backed by a firm hope in the blessings of the future."

Unremitting prayer is the death of despondency.

Part IV

The Physical Passions

Step 14

Gluttony

Gluttony is hypocrisy of the stomach. Filled, it moans about scarcity; stuffed, and crammed, it wails about its hunger. Gluttony thinks up seasonings, creates sweet recipes. Stop up one urge and another bursts out; stop that one and you unleash yet another. Gluttony has a deceptive appearance: it eats moderately but wants to gobble everything at the same time.

What comes to mind when you hear the word *gluttony*? You probably think of someone overweight eating large quantities of food. One might even think that, outside the fasting periods, this is quite acceptable. After all, if an Orthodox Christian observes all the fasts, he spends about half the year fasting. So perhaps you might think fasters are entitled to feast when it is permitted.

But as a passion, gluttony is a little more complicated than this. For passions are not mere actions, but conditions of soul and body that distort our relationship not only with our fellow human beings, but also with our natural environment and our own bodies.

It is interesting that St. John, on more than one occasion, uses the term "gluttonous soul" or "gluttonous spirit." While we are speaking of what is commonly thought of as a physical sin, the distinction between physical and spiritual is an oversimplification. We cannot make such a sharp distinction between body and soul, since there is nothing human beings can do without both of these together. Thus physical sins have a spiritual dimension.

The *Ladder* gives us a good example of how a gluttonous spirit distorts our approach not only to food, but also to the feasts and fasts of the Church. St. John writes:

> **The gluttonous monk celebrates on Saturdays and Sundays.[18] He counts the days to Easter, and for days in advance he gets the food ready. The slave of the belly ponders the menu with which to celebrate the feast.**

Orthodox Christians often spend fasting periods groaning about food. And not only this—some become so obsessive about observing the rules of the fast that they spend a great deal of time examining ingredients when they go shopping and are constantly thinking about what they can and cannot eat. The result is that they end up being more concerned with food during the fasts than they are the rest of the time, which contradicts one of the purposes of fasting: to attach less significance to food, not more.

18 The normal discipline is that fasting on Saturdays and Sundays during the austere fasting period of Great Lent is less rigorous than on the other days of the week, and wine and oil are permitted on these days. The only Saturday of the year that is reckoned a strict fast is Great and Holy Saturday. For an explanation of the reason behind the relaxation of fasting on these days, read St. John Cassian's *Institutes* 2:18 and 3:9.

Furthermore, fasters can sometimes find themselves concentrating more on what they will eat once the fast is over than on the meaning of the feast for which the fast prepares us. When the feast arrives, be it Pascha, the Nativity, the Dormition, or the Feast of Saints Peter and Paul, we consider gluttony to be perfectly acceptable. We stuff our faces with all the things we have spent many weeks fasting from.

This mentality can be recognized not only in the lengthier periods of fasting, but even on a weekly basis. Many of those who observe the Wednesday and Friday fasts tend to think of every other day as a feast in terms of food. A vivid example of this has stayed with me:

> There was once a priest who was invited to supper on a day that was not a fast day. He was served a fairly simple dish of vegetables. He seemed rather distressed and blurted out, "It's not a fast day today!" The poor woman who made the meal was quite upset. She was accustomed to simple eating, but now she felt she had done something wrong. The priest offended a simple, kind, and devout woman in the name of "religious observance" because of his gluttonous spirit.

This is what happens when we have a gluttonous soul. We spend five days a week thinking we are entitled to gorge ourselves on the foods not permitted on Wednesdays and Fridays. This is because even if we observe the rules of the fasts strictly, even if we normally discipline ourselves in our eating habits, we have nonetheless not overcome the passion of gluttony.

A gluttonous spirit craves food. It regards fasting as deprivation and therefore sees all other times as opportunities to make up for that deprivation. It considers high-quality food, or eating meat five days a week, to be something to which it is entitled. This passion of gluttony therefore distorts the balance of the Church's discipline of fasting and feasting in moderation. A gluttonous soul looks forward more to a banquet at Pascha than it does to the powerful life-shaping celebration of Christ's Resurrection. It turns the church year into an endless cycle of gluttony and deprivation, binging and purging.

The Church's tradition of fasting exists to restore balance between body and soul, between penitence and rejoicing, between us and the world around us. If fasting from food is, as the Orthodox Church teaches, only the means to an end, and not the end in itself, then so too feasting with food is only the means to enhancing our joy; it should not become the center of our celebration.

St. John is therefore careful to endorse moderation in both feasting and fasting. One may have the impression that moderation does not characterize his approach at all, for he criticizes priests who permit those not under their spiritual counsel to observe relaxations of fasting on feast days (wine and oil, or fish on Great Feasts that fall within the period of Lent, such as the Annunciation and Palm Sunday). In fact, this may be the reason some enthusiasts frown upon eating fish on the Annunciation during Lent or on Palm Sunday.

But these relaxations on feast days that coincide with fast days were established by the Church for good reason. If we consider food to be something important enough to fast from in Lent, then it is also important enough to be part of the joy of Great Feasts. Food is not something profane that has no bearing on our spiritual well-being. Food is actually more important than many Christians like to think. There can be no true spiritual life that does not involve the body. Food is not simply fuel to keep us going. It can bring gladness, warmth, comfort, strength, and health; and it can have the opposite effects when it is abused. To let Great Feasts pass us by when it comes to food, as though the feasts are of no significance, is to lose the fullness of spiritual life and of Christian celebration.

St. John's appeal to moderation is made clear in his criticism of Abba Evagrius (despite being condemned as a heretic, his spiritual writings have an important place in Orthodox spirituality). Evagrius recommended taking only bread and water to counter the desire for different foods. St. John says this is **like telling a child to climb the entire ladder in a single stride.** It is better to fast moderately throughout the Church's appointed fasting periods than it is to fast so austerely that we give up the effort altogether within a few days. St. John recommends a much more sensible approach:

> **When our soul wants different foods, it is looking for what is proper to its nature . . . what we ought to do is to deny ourselves fattening foods, then foods that warm us up, then whatever happens to make our food especially pleasant. Give yourself food that is satisfying and easily**

digestible, thereby counteracting endless hunger by giving yourself plenty.

Because food is a part of spiritual life, and not something that falls outside the realm of spirituality, fasting has always been an important element of Christian practice. It is also the reason religious celebrations are marked by feasting. If done in a spirit of humility, love, sacrifice, and moderation, fasting can make a big difference to our frame of mind and to our prayer. For instead of the body becoming a hindrance, it is mastered and subjected to the will of the spirit:

Fasting ends lust, roots out bad thoughts . . . makes for purity of prayer, an enlightened soul, a watchful mind. . . . Fasting is the door of compunction, humble sighing, joyful contrition, an end to chatter, an occasion for silence, a custodian of obedience, a lightening of sleep, health of the body, an agent of dispassion, a remission of sins, the gate, indeed, the delight of Paradise.

Step 15

Lust and Chastity

Chastity is a supernatural denial of what one is by nature, so that a mortal and corruptible body is competing in a truly marvelous way with incorporeal spirits. A chaste man is someone who has driven out bodily love by means of divine love, who has used heavenly fire to quench the fires of the flesh.

People tend to think of chastity in purely sexual terms—as the virtue opposed to sexual depravity. But it has a deeper meaning than this. It is worth noting that in the Orthodox marriage service, we pray that the newlyweds may live in "chastity" (in Greek, *sophrosini*). Yet in the very same service, we pray numerous times that they may have honorable children. How can a couple live in chastity (sexual purity) and yet have children?

To answer this we must consider that a fuller, more accurate translation of *sophrosini* is whole-mindedness. It is ultimately harmony between body and soul, between the flesh and the spirit—a state of mind in which the two do not war with each other, but work together as one. Thus St. John writes that **chastity is a name common to all virtues.** He goes on to say: **The chaste man is not someone with a body undefiled but rather a person whose members are in complete subjection to the soul.**

Chastity must not, therefore, be understood in terms of celibacy, but in terms of control over one's sexual impulses. Within marriage, sex is blessed. It is not only for procreation—it is also an expression of love. There is nothing impure about a married couple enjoying sex. Marriage is not usually a calling for those who are called to celibacy. As our Lord said:

> "There are eunuchs who were born thus from *their* mother's womb, and there are eunuchs who were made eunuchs by men, and there are eunuchs who have made themselves eunuchs for the kingdom of heaven's sake. He who is able to accept *it*, let him accept *it*." (Matt. 19:12)[19]

But within an Orthodox marriage, there are boundaries. Just as food is not in itself sinful, but abuse of food is, so too sex is not in itself sinful. But when sex becomes disconnected from its purpose—when it ceases to be something blessed by the Church, an expression of the intimate union between husband and wife, who are a living symbol of the union between Christ (the Bridegroom) and the Church (His Bride)—it alienates us from God and from a correct relationship with one another and with our own bodies. Orthodoxy expects sexual relations to be between one man and one woman within marriage.

19 Here our Lord is using the word *eunuch* as a metaphor for "celibate."

But it is precisely on this point that many Christians face a serious dilemma. As we saw above, Christ points out that not everyone is called to a life of celibacy. It is worth noting that in biblical times, couples were married at a very early age indeed (usually by the age of thirteen or fourteen). Premarital sex in biblical times was practically impossible, for by the time sexual impulses kicked in, a man and woman were already married.

But today, countless Christians who are not called to a life of celibacy end up struggling with this natural impulse throughout their teens and even into their twenties and thirties and beyond. While we must not abandon the Christian understanding that sex outside of marriage is not in accordance with God's will, we must also have compassion on those who struggle with sexual desire. For not all are called to sexual celibacy. This is why St. John advises those who are called to it not to think they have conquered this passion by their own efforts:

> **Anyone trained in chastity should give himself no credit for any achievements, for a man cannot conquer what he actually is. When nature is overcome, it should be admitted that this is due to Him Who is above nature, since it cannot be denied that the weaker always yields to the stronger.**
>
> **Do not imagine that you will overwhelm the demon of fornication by entering into an argument. Nature is on his side and he has the best of the argument. So the man who decides to struggle against his flesh and to overcome it by his own efforts is fighting in vain. The truth is that**

> **unless the Lord overturns the house of the flesh and builds the house of the soul, the man wishing to overcome it has watched and fasted for nothing. Offer up to the Lord the weakness of your nature. Admit your incapacity and, without your knowing it, you will win for yourself the gift of chastity.**

Chastity must not be understood only in terms of physical abstinence from sex. As our Lord said, "Whoever looks at a woman to lust for her has already committed adultery with her in his heart" (Matt. 5:28). This does not mean it is a sin to be attracted to someone, to acknowledge or admire his or her beauty. It means that if circumstance is the only thing that prevents us from acting on sexual sin, then in the eyes of God this is no different from actually committing the act:

> **I have seen men who lapsed against their will and I have seen men who would willingly lapse but are unable to do so. These I pity far more than the daily sinner, for though impotent they long for corruption.**

The *Ladder* provides a wonderful example of how St. Nonnus, bishop of Heliopolis, was not oblivious to beauty, but perceived it in such a holy and innocent way that it was cause for him to weep with love for God's wonderful creation:

> **There was a man who, having looked on a body of great beauty, at once gave praise to its Creator and after one look was stirred to love God and to weep copiously, so that it was marvelous how something that could have brought**

low one person managed to be the cause of a heavenly crown for another.

Dreams, Fantasies, and Emissions

Because St. John is writing for monks, a good deal of his chapter on chastity is dedicated to nocturnal emissions (wet dreams) and impure thoughts. I would not like to spend too much time on this subject, but a few words ought to be said about it. While the emissions young men experience in sleep should not be regarded as sinful (St. John considers them **an accident, which of course is free from sin**), at the same time, he does regard them as problematic, but also as something that can be controlled, for he considers them a result of high living and gluttony. St. John frequently connects gluttony with sexual impurity, and he considers abstinence from food as an aid to overcoming sexual instincts and emissions. But St. John also speaks of **dreamless emissions.** It is possible that he is referring to masturbation, but this is not altogether clear:

> **The beginning of chastity is refusal to consent to evil thoughts and occasional dreamless emissions; the middle stage is to be free of dreams and emissions even when there are natural movements of the body brought on by eating too much; the completion of chastity comes when mortified thoughts are followed by a mortified body.**
>
> **A sign of real chastity is to be unaffected by the dreams that come with sleep. Equally, a sign of complete sensuality is to be liable to emissions from bad thoughts even when one is awake.**

Among beginners lapses usually occur because of high living, something that, together with arrogance, brings down also those who have made some progress. But among those nearing perfection, a lapse is solely due to the fact of passing judgment on one's neighbor.

Far more problematic than dreams are fantasies. The devil uses these very effectively. God gives us reality; the devil gives us fantasy. And of course fantasy is always a disappointment. People can end up never being satisfied. So they conclude the problem is their partner. They look for someone who can sate their desires, but of course this never really happens. They end up basing their expectations of sex on pornography. So they become curious about more depraved sexual acts or multiple partners. They develop **a yearning for bodies.**

But the fantasies are never satisfied because they are nothing but fantasies. The devil is a liar. He likes to make us think we are missing out on something truly incredible, but the reality is we are not missing out on anything real. And so we can waste our whole lives searching and hoping for things that do not exist or that, in the end, only leave us with a sense of disappointment, shame, and guilt.

Even with those who have never engaged in sexual activity, the devil likes to use curiosity to make us fall. And if we do, then he says, "Well, that was just the first time. It is never fantastic the first time. It gets so much better. Try again." As St. John describes it:

> **The serpent of sensuality has many faces. To those who have had no experience of sin he suggests the idea of trying it once and then stopping. Then the crafty creature, exploiting the recollection of having sinned once, urges them to try again.**

The Vicious Cycle of Sin

Apart from fantasy, there are two ways in which the demons use lust against devout Christians. To lead us into sin, they try to persuade us of God's mercy. "After all, sex is perfectly natural. God surely would not hold such sin against you. You cannot help what you are." But after we commit the sin, they try to make us despair, to make us think it is the worst sin that can be committed, that we are depraved and incapable of salvation because we do not have the strength to overcome our nature. Then, if we have been convinced of God's mercy and forgiveness, the process begins all over again, leaving us going round in circles in a vicious cycle of sin, despair, and forgiveness:

> **Our relentless enemy, the teacher of fornication, whispers that God is lenient and particularly merciful to this passion, since it is so very natural. Yet if we watch the wiles of the demons we will observe that after we have actually sinned they will affirm that God is a just and inexorable judge. They say one thing to lead us into sin, another thing to overwhelm us in despair. And if we are sorrowful or inclined to despair, we are slower to sin again, but when the sorrow and the despair have been quenched, the tyrannical demon begins to speak to us again of God's mercy.**

What Can We Do?

What can we do to gain any mastery of this desire if we are not married, especially if we are not called to the celibate life? St. John recommends contemplation of death and the Jesus Prayer: "Lord Jesus Christ, Son of God, have mercy on me, a sinner."

> **So let the remembrance of death and the concise Jesus Prayer go to sleep with you and get up with you, for nothing helps you as these do when you are asleep.**

The beauty and practicality of this prayer is that, being a simple and concise invocation that can be repeated as often as we wish—either audibly or silently—it can be prayed at all times, in all places, in all situations. Whether we are sick in bed, waiting for the bus, stuck in a traffic jam, bored rigid in a dull committee meeting, or alone at home, we can dart up this prayer to God when all other prayers are impossible.

To constantly have this prayer in our minds, in our hearts, and on our lips can help drive out impure thoughts. It is particularly useful when we lie down to sleep, when we are most prone to sexual thoughts and urges. Go to bed repeating this prayer constantly. Let us think of our beds as our graves. Let us consider the possibility that we will not wake in the morning. Make prayer the last thing you do before you doze off, and the first thing you do when you wake up. Also, crying out to God in our own words, when the struggle seems too great, is something God receives with compassion:

Cry out to God, Who has the strength to save you. Do not bother with elegant and clever words. Just speak humbly, beginning with, "Have mercy on me, for I am weak" (Ps. 6:3).

Another piece of advice is to seek the counsel of our spiritual father or of devout Christian friends—**a spiritual director or a helpful brother, old in wisdom rather than years**—not one who is too spiritually immature to deal with sexual matters in a compassionate and understanding manner, not someone who is scandalized by such sin, but one who will take your struggles seriously and give you realistic advice and guidance in mastering your own sexuality.

The Human Body

Christian spiritual teachings, particularly monastic writings, may often appear to present the human body as an enemy, as something to be despised. But our bodies are as much a part of us as are our souls. Without our bodies, we can do no good. Our flesh has been sanctified and marked for deification due to our Lord's Incarnation, death, and Resurrection. Yet, as St. Paul says:

> I find then a law, that evil is present with me, the one who wills to do good. For I delight in the law of God according to the inward man. But I see another law in my members, warring against the law of my mind, and bringing me into captivity to the law of sin which is in my members. O wretched man that I am! Who will deliver me from this body of death? (Rom. 7:21–24)

In a similar way, St. John, in a moving passage in the *Ladder*, describes his own inner conflict, his love-hate relationship with his body:

> By what rule or manner can I bind this body of mine? By what precedent can I judge him? Before I can bind him he is let loose, before I condemn him I am reconciled to him, before I can punish him I bow down to him and feel sorry for him. How can I hate him when my nature disposes me to love him? How can I break away from him when I am bound to him forever? How can I escape from him when he is going to rise with me? How can I make him incorruptible when he has received a corruptible nature? How can I argue with him when all the arguments of nature are on his side? . . . He is my helper and my enemy, my assistant and my opponent, a protector and a traitor. I am kind to him and he assaults me. If I wear him out he gets weak. If he has a rest he becomes unruly. If I upset him he cannot stand it. If I mortify him I endanger myself. If I strike him down I have nothing left by which to acquire virtues. I embrace him. And I turn away from him.
>
> What is this mystery in me? What is the principle of this mixture of body and soul? How can I be my own friend and my own enemy?

The main principle of the ascetic life is to make the body our friend rather than our enemy. It must be trained and disciplined, and taught to love and serve the soul, to be a temple of the Holy Spirit. While sexual desire may seem at times impossible to overcome, lust herself reveals that she can be conquered:

"Within me is my begetter, the love of self. The fire that comes from outside is too much pampering and care. The fire within me is past ease and things long done . . . if you have learned the sure and rooted weakness within both you and me, you have manacled my hands. If you starve your longings, you have bound my feet, and they can travel no further. If you have taken up the yoke of obedience, you have cast my yoke aside. If you have taken possession of humility, you have cut off my head."

This is the fifteenth reward of victory. He who has earned it while still alive has died and been resurrected. From now on he has a taste of the immortality to come.

Step 16

Avarice

Avarice is a worship of idols and is the offspring of unbelief. . . . The miser sneers at the gospel and is a deliberate transgressor. The man of charity spreads his money about him, but the man who claims to possess both charity and money is a self-deceived fool.

How much is too much? Where is the dividing line between what I need and what I want? This problem applies not only to gluttony, but to all material needs, particularly money. Just as gluttony is the passion that distorts our definition of need in terms of food and drink, avarice is the passion that distorts our definition of need in terms of money and luxury.

The first principle of Christian charity is that we should give in accordance with our ability. What matters in God's eyes is not how much we give, but how much we sacrifice. As many Church Fathers have said, to give from our poverty is more valuable in God's eyes than to give from our abundance. This is because the underlying principle of Christian charity is self-denying love. As St. Basil the Great writes, "Are you poor? You know someone who is even poorer. . . . Do not shrink from giving the little you have; do not prefer your own benefit to remedying the common distress."[20]

However, this simple principle of giving what we can is complicated by the way we adjust our definition of need to suit the desire to satisfy our passions. We tend to think of luxuries as necessities. We think that we need to eat extremely well, that we really do need that expensive pair of shoes, or that we need to have abundant savings for a rainy day. This temptation is often worse for those with children. Obviously married people need to provide for their children's needs—food, clothing, education, and so on. But it is a great temptation for them to use the love of their children as an excuse to satisfy a desire for a luxurious and privileged lifestyle. It can also lead to spoiling our children rotten. Again in the words of St. Basil:

> "But wealth is necessary for rearing children," someone will say. This is a specious excuse for greed; although you speak as though children were your concern, you betray the inclinations of your own heart. Do not impute guilt to the guiltless! They have their own Master who cares for their needs. They received their being from God, and God will provide what they need to live. Was the command found in the Gospel, "If you wish to be perfect, sell your possessions and give the money to the poor," not written for the married?

20 *On Social Justice*, trans. Fr. C. Paul Schroeder (Crestwood, NY: SVS Press, 2009), p. 83.

After seeking the blessing of children from the Lord, and being found worthy to become parents, did you at once add the following, "Give me children, that I might disobey your commandments; give me children, that I might not attain the Kingdom of Heaven"?[21]

St. John Chrysostom reminds us that it is not wealth, but the abuse of wealth, that is evil:

Wealth will be good for the possessor if he does not spend it only on luxury, or on strong drink and harmful pleasures; if he enjoys luxury in moderation and distributes the rest to the stomachs of the poor, then wealth is a good thing.[22]

Yet St. John of the Ladder warns us that even the idea of charity—the desire to have plenty in order to give to others—can be little more than an excuse for avarice:

Do not say you are interested in money for the sake of the poor, for two mites were sufficient to purchase the kingdom (cf. Luke 21:2). . . . The pretext of almsgiving is the beginning of avarice, and the finish is detestation of the poor. The collector is stirred by charity, but, when the money is in, the grip tightens.

The demon of avarice fights hard against those who have nothing. When it fails to overcome them, it begins to tell them about the wretched conditions of the poor, thereby inducing those in the religious life to become concerned once more with material things.

21 *On Social Justice, op. cit.,*. p. 54.
22 *On Wealth and Poverty,* trans. Catharine P. Roth (Crestwood, NY: SVS Press, 1984), pp. 136–137.

How little the rich really do give, compared to what they could give, hanging onto wealth in order to maintain their luxurious lifestyles! Again, St. Basil also touches upon this issue—how our passions limit and distort our perception of how much we can give:

> How many could you have delivered from want with but a single ring from your finger? How many households fallen into destitution might you have raised? In just one of our closets there are enough clothes to cover an entire town shivering with cold.[23]

A good friend once aptly noted that this passage reminded him of *Schindler's List,* when Schindler realizes:

> "I could have got more out. I could have got more. . . . I threw away so much money. You have no idea! This car! O God, what about the car? Why did I keep the car? Ten people right there. . . . This pen—two more people. This is gold—two more people. . . . I could have got one more person, and I didn't. I didn't!"[24]

The more we love our neighbor as ourselves—the more, in other words, we feel the needs of others as though they are our own—the less inclined we will be to consider our luxuries as more important than our neighbor's basic needs. "The more you abound in wealth, the more you lack in love."[25]

---

23 *On Social Justice, op. cit.,* p. 46.

24 http://logismoitouaaron.blogspot.co.uk/2010/03/on-social-justice-by-st-basil-great.html (accessed on 12/7/2012).

25 *On Social Justice, op. cit.,* p. 43.

Step 17

Poverty

The man who has tasted the things of heaven daily thinks nothing of what is below, but he who has had no taste of heaven finds pleasure in possessions.

At the end of the previous chapter I concluded that love remedies avarice. But love is a word Christians throw around a great deal. All the time I hear people say, "Love is all that matters," or something to that effect. But rarely do we consider that love is not that easy. Love is the final step of the Ladder, not the first.

One could say the whole battle of Christian life, the very purpose of asceticism, is to acquire divine love. This is why St. John follows his chapter on the passion of avarice (the fruit of selfishness) with a chapter on the virtue of poverty (the fruit of self-denying love). It may seem strange to people that poverty is reckoned a virtue. We are inclined to think of poverty as nothing more than not having enough to get by. But here St. John is speaking of voluntary poverty. And this ties in with what we said at the end of the last chapter. As St. Basil writes:

> Those who love their neighbor as themselves possess nothing more than their neighbor; yet surely, you seem to have great possessions! How else can this be, but that you have preferred your own enjoyment to the consolation of many?[26]

Here we see the principle of Christian love as ascesis. Without the latter, we are too weak to endure hardship and sacrifice for the sake of others. We must discipline ourselves through ascetic struggle to overcome the passions of avarice and gluttony. Then we will discover that we have much more to give to others than we thought. Many may think the principle of charity is that the more we have, the more we can give. But as St. John points out, having much does not necessarily mean we will give much. The principle of Christian charity is not the more we have, the more we give; but rather, the less we need, the more we give. This is the meaning of poverty as a virtue. It is **resignation from care . . . life without anxiety.**

St. John Chrysostom reminds us that those who practice voluntary poverty are the ones who are truly rich, because they are free of need and worldly concerns:

> If you see someone greedy for many things, you should consider him the poorest of all, even if he has acquired everyone's money. If, on the other hand, you see someone with few needs, you should count him the richest of all, even if he has acquired nothing. For we are accustomed to judge

---

26 *Ibid.*

> poverty and affluence by the disposition of the mind, not by the measure of one's substance.[27]

In a similar way, St. John of the Ladder says the Christian who has mastered the virtue of poverty

> **has handed all cares over to God. . . . If he lacks something he does not complain to his fellows and he accepts what comes his way as if from the hand of the Lord. In his poverty he turns into a son of detachment and he sets no value on what he has. Having withdrawn from the world, he comes to regard everything as refuse. Indeed he is not genuinely poor if he starts to worry about something.**

The less attached to the things of this world we become, the more we discover inner peace and true freedom:

> **The man who thinks nothing of goods has freed himself from quarrels and disputes.**

By contrast, the more attached to worldly things we become, the more we come into conflict with one another:

> **Avarice is said to be the root of all evil (1 Tim. 6:10), and it is so. Because it causes hatred, theft, envy, separations, hostility, stormy blasts, remembrance of past wrongs, inhuman acts and even murder.**

We said that poverty, in spiritual life, is a virtue, but the state of poverty in and of itself does not usually lead to peace and freedom from worldly needs and desires, but the exact opposite. The

27 *On Wealth and Poverty*, *op. cit.*, p. 40.

evils caused by avarice mentioned above tend to become more acute in times of poverty. This is because someone who is poor can still be avaricious, and the greater his poverty, the more desperate he becomes to acquire what he needs or desires.

Voluntary poverty is a virtue because it is an expression of self-denying love: through ascesis we are able to live a frugal life, enabling us to give more to others. Poverty is therefore a sacrifice of the will, a surrender of our worldly desires for love of God and neighbor. That is why poverty is the virtue that overcomes avarice:

> **The man who gives up possessions for religious motives is great, but the man who renounces his will is holy indeed; the one will earn money or grace a hundred times over, but the other will inherit eternal life.**

Part V

The Spiritual Passions (Continued)

Step 18

Insensitivity/ Lack of Awareness

Insensitivity is a deadened feeling in body and spirit, and comes from long sickness and carelessness. Lack of awareness is negligence that has become a habit. It is thought gone numb, an offspring of predisposition, a trap for zeal, a noose for courage, an ignorance of compunction, the gateway to despair, the mother of forgetfulness giving birth to loss of fear of God and, in turn, to a deadened spirit.

The word *insensitivity* as St. John uses it does not mean what we normally call insensitivity. When we say someone is insensitive, we usually mean he does not consider other people's feelings. But this is not what it means in spiritual life. It is best understood as a deep-rooted hypocrisy. It is a hypocrisy so deep that it becomes almost impossible to recognize it in ourselves, though, of course, we are quick to condemn it in others.

Step Eighteen is my favorite chapter of the *Ladder,* and in loving and praising it I find myself guilty of the very passion St. John is describing.

The insensitive man is a foolish philosopher, an exegete condemned by his own words, a scholar who contradicts himself, a blind man teaching sight to others. . . . He talks profoundly about death and acts as if he will never die. . . . He has plenty to say about self-control and fights for a gourmet life. He reads about the judgment and begins to smile, about vainglory and is vainglorious while he is reading. He recites what he has learnt about keeping vigil, and at once drops off to sleep. Prayer he extols, and runs from it as if from a plague. Blessings he showers on obedience, and is the first to disobey. Detachment he praises, and he shamelessly fights over a rag. . . . He blesses silence and cannot stop talking about it. He teaches meekness and frequently gets angry while he is teaching it. . . . In front of others he criticizes himself for being vainglorious, and in making the admission he is looking for glory. . . . Out in the world he is full of praise for the solitary life and cannot see how much he is disgracing himself. He glorifies almsgivers and despises the poor.

This chapter spoke to me more powerfully and truthfully than anything else I have read. I speak constantly of repentance, but my life is bare of its fruits. I teach others how to fast, but I do not put what I teach into practice. I speak of self-control as a Christian virtue, yet there are atheists who practice it better than I do. I praise humility though I have none. And in confessing this, I want others to admire my humility. I am writing this book only to discover that in doing so, I condemn myself. I criticize others for criticizing others, and I speak about people behind their back for doing the very thing I am doing myself.

And do I go home that very evening and fall on my knees in tears to beg God to forgive me? No! Because I am insensitive. How is it possible that I am not flooding my bed with tears every night for my sins? How is it possible that I am not willing to deprive myself of comfort and satisfaction for just a small taste of sanctity? I do not acknowledge the severity of my sins; I do not wish to be what I claim I wish to be. And admitting my hypocrisy does not make me act upon it. No matter how much I confess my sin, no matter how guilty I feel, however much I yearn for holiness, I am too lazy and indifferent to go through the arduous struggle holiness demands.

Even when I celebrate the Divine Liturgy, I find myself guilty of this insensitivity. How often have I spoken to others of the life-changing power of the Eucharist, while I have remained completely unchanged by it! Those who are, like me, insensitive **are stony, hard, and blinded. In front of the altar they feel nothing. They receive the Holy Gift as if it were ordinary bread.**

This insensitivity to our own wretched condition so blinds us that we can only recognize our sins when we are forced to see ourselves in others. Every sinner is a mirror of another. This is why parables are often used in the Scriptures: to show us our own behavior in stories about other people. Take, for example, King David. He slept with a man's wife and got her pregnant. When he realized it was impossible to conceal the identity of the child's father, he had the husband killed. One day, the Prophet Nathan tells the king the following story:

> "There were two men in one city, one rich and the other poor. The rich *man* had exceedingly many flocks and herds. But the poor *man* had nothing, except one little ewe lamb which he had bought and nourished; and it grew up together with him and with his children. It ate of his own food and drank from his own cup and lay in his bosom; and it was like a daughter to him. And a traveler came to the rich man, who refused to take from his own flock and from his own herd to prepare one for the wayfaring man who had come to him; but he took the poor man's lamb and prepared it for the man who had come to him." So David's anger was greatly aroused against the man, and he said to Nathan, "As the LORD lives, the man who has done this shall surely die! And he shall restore fourfold for the lamb, because he did this thing and because he had no pity." Then Nathan said to David, "You *are* the man!" (2 Kingdoms [2 Samuel]:12:1–7)

Only then, after he had passed judgment on himself and recognized himself in the rich man in that story, did David repent of his sin.

Our Lord used parables in exactly the same way. One example should be sufficient:

> "There was a certain landowner who planted a vineyard and set a hedge around it, dug a winepress in it and built a tower. And he leased it to vinedressers and went into a far country. Now when vintage-time drew near, he sent his servants to the vinedressers, that they might receive its fruit. And the vinedressers took his servants, beat one, killed one, and stoned another. Again he sent other servants, more than the first, and they did likewise to them. Then last of all he sent

his son to them, saying, 'They will respect my son.' But when the vinedressers saw the son, they said among themselves, 'This is the heir. Come, let us kill him and seize his inheritance.' So they took him and cast *him* out of the vineyard and killed *him*. Therefore, when the owner of the vineyard comes, what will he do to those vinedressers?" They said to Him, "He will destroy those wicked men miserably, and lease *his* vineyard to other vinedressers who will render to him the fruits in their seasons." (Matt. 21:33–41)

The Pharisees passed a severe and just judgment on the villains of the parable. In so doing they condemned themselves, for without realizing it, they were the villains in the story. People sometimes complain about the notion of Divine Judgment. "How can God judge and condemn us if He loves us?" But we condemn ourselves every time we judge others. With each thought and word with which we condemn sin, we create more rope to hang ourselves with. "For by your words you will be justified, and by your words you will be condemned" (Matt. 12:37).

This insensitivity appears to have no means of defeat. If a hypocrite seeks to overcome his passions by fasting, he becomes proud and judgmental. If a proud man tries to be humble, he becomes proud of his humility. If he prays, he thinks he has achieved something. If he reads, he thinks he has become an expert on what he has read. If he acknowledges his hypocrisy, he thinks he has mastered humility, for insensitivity is **the ally of Fake Piety.** Every cure for insensitivity seems to become absorbed in the very sin it is supposed to remedy. There seems to be no escape.

All of this may sound hopeless, and in a way, it is. Because for as long as we think we can overcome hypocrisy by our own works, there is no hope. "Who then can be saved?" (Luke 18:26). If we can recognize that hopelessness in ourselves, if we cry to God with all sincerity and desperation, knowing there is no hope in anything else, then we can turn hopelessness into hope. "The things which are impossible with men are possible with God" (Luke 18:27).

Step 19

Sleep, Prayer, and Church

Sleep is a natural state. It is also an image of death and a respite of the senses. Sleep is one, but like desire it has many sources. That is to say, it comes from nature, from food, from demons, or perhaps in some degree even from prolonged fasting by which the flesh is moved to long for repose.

One of the principles of monastic life is to imitate as far as possible the angels, the "bodiless powers of heaven," as they are often called in the Orthodox Church. And this means to overcome, as far as possible, the limitations of the flesh. The angels do not eat or sleep. They forever and without ceasing praise and worship God. Therefore, our beloved monks and nuns in their monasteries strive to imitate this angelic life as far as possible by reducing how much they eat and sleep in order to dedicate as much time as possible to prayer and worship, and to keep their bodies under the control and will of the spirit. Thus in monastic life, sleep, like food, is something that must be curbed, taking only what is needed to keep the body going.

Just as too much drinking comes from habit, so too from habit comes overindulgence in sleep. For this reason one has to struggle against it especially at the start of one's religious life, because a long-standing habit is very difficult to correct.

While the rest of us cannot hope to dedicate exclusively to prayer and worship anywhere near as much time as monks and nuns can, we can certainly train ourselves not to waste more time than we need in bed.

Sleep is, of course, a perfectly natural thing. There is nothing remotely sinful about it. In fact, apart from snorers, even the most horrid people seem pleasant when they are sleeping. But while we cannot do evil while asleep, neither can we do good. **Excessive sleep is a bad companion, stealing half a lifetime or more from the lazy man.**

You may have noticed that this chapter has been placed under the category of spiritual passions. This may seem curious to many. We do not tend to think of sleep as a spiritual thing. But just as too much food affects the condition of the soul, so too does too much sleep. Furthermore, when a passion comes into conflict with our spiritual life, distinctions between physical and spiritual are irrelevant. Body and soul together: that is the principle of asceticism; that is the only way spiritual life can even be possible. Ever tried going to church without taking your body with you? And this is precisely why the desire for too much sleep is a spiritual passion.

We are not talking about physical tiredness; we are not talking about what the body needs (and the need of each person is different). What I am talking about is priorities. I have said before that when it comes to things we consider important, when we know we have to be somewhere at a certain time, we make sure we get up in time to do so (though now and again we may oversleep). But many of us do not apply the same urgency to prayer and worship. This is why the subject of sleep is treated in connection with prayer and participation in church services.

St. John describes how laziness can cut into our spiritual life in a way we can all understand even today: **Wait until the first hymns are over. . . . Then it will be time enough to go to church.** And that was before the invention of snooze buttons!

The saints live for prayer and worship. If they could, they would not sleep at all in order to keep praying. Indeed, this is the purpose of vigils. I have been fortunate enough to experience all-night vigils on several occasions, both in monasteries and in parish churches. Strangely enough, they are more invigorating than they are grueling. It is a pity there are not more of them in parish churches.

No one, not even saints, can live without sleep. But if we truly love prayer (especially when we know that work and other obligations will be devouring a good deal of our time), we can spend a little less time in bed so that we can spend a little more time at prayer. The more the flesh is disciplined and subjected to the will of the spirit, the easier this becomes.

However, tiredness or lack of sleep can affect our prayer. It is surely better to get a reasonable amount of sleep and spend less time praying, but with an alert and focused mind, than to deprive ourselves of sleep only to stand there trying to pray while half awake. While this is true, we must consider whether it is tiredness or despondency that is interfering with our prayer. But whatever the case, a more acute perception of God's presence is the remedy for that problem:

> **The man who considers with sensitivity of heart that he is standing before God will be an immovable pillar in prayer.**

What do we consider important enough to stay awake and alert for? I have sometimes been so enthralled by a late-night movie on the television that I've forced myself to stay awake till the end, although I wanted sleep. I chose one spiritually unprofitable activity over another. Shouldn't I choose more important things than a movie over sleep? Shouldn't I do the same for prayer?

As Christ in the Garden of Gethsemane awaited His pending arrest, torture, and death, He commanded His disciples to stay awake and pray, but they kept falling asleep (Matt. 26:36–46). Christ asks us to do the same, but we too keep failing, for "the spirit indeed *is* willing, but the flesh *is* weak" (Matt. 26:41).

Why is it that the spirit, which is strong, is overpowered by the flesh, which is weak? It is because we are not sensitive to the presence of God. We give the flesh what it wants and starve the spirit of what it needs. If only we could sense and perceive His presence every morning, every night, every day!

When I was a child, sometimes a relative or family friend would make a rare visit to our home, but I was sent to bed. Only I did not wish to go to sleep, because I wanted to be with the guest. When I woke up, I hurried to get out of bed to greet the visitor. I should have the same enthusiasm for prayer. If I could learn to feel the presence of the Holy Spirit as tangibly as I could feel the presence of that guest, I would not love sleep so much, and I would not need it as much as I think I do.

Step 20

Alertness

Some keep nightlong vigil, their hands raised in prayer like spirits free of every burden. Others sing the psalms or read, while some, out of weakness, bravely fight sleep by working with their hands. Others think constantly of death and try in this way to obtain a contrite heart. Of all these types, the first and last persevere in nightlong vigil out of love of God, the second do what is appropriate for a monk, and the third travel the lowliest road. Still, God accepts and judges the offerings of each type in accordance with their intentions and their abilities.

From the passion of sleep we move on to its positive counterpart: the virtue of alertness. It is a virtue because it is a state of being in which we are always prepared to meet our Maker. This principle of vigilance is made explicit in Holy Week:

> *Behold, the Bridegroom comes at midnight, and blessed is the servant whom He shall find watching. And again, unworthy is the servant whom He shall find heedless. Beware, therefore, O my soul, do not be weighed down with sleep, lest you be given up to death, and lest you be*

shut out of the kingdom. But rouse yourself, crying, "Holy, holy, holy are You, our God."[28]

If the purpose of alertness, or vigilance, is always to be prepared to meet the Lord and not to waste the time we have been given for repentance, then prayer or spiritual study, especially the reading of the Scriptures, should be the activities that fill those waking hours otherwise wasted on sleep. But the reality is that the majority do not waste too much time sleeping, but on the contrary, don't get enough of it. Those with babies and small children know this all too well, while for most people a normal job does not permit excessive sleep.

But this brings us back again to the issue of priorities. Do we see it as a necessity to wake up on a Saturday or Sunday morning, when (in some cases) we do not need to go to work, in order to go to church or say our prayers? Of course, we should be careful not to push ourselves too far. We all get tired. We all need rest. But the fundamental spiritual question remains: Why do we not have that same sense of urgency and alertness when it comes to spiritual life? We feel there is no practical consequence to skipping morning prayer or not going to church. There is no penalty. We are not going to lose our job or be reprimanded. So there is no sense of "I have to" about such things.

Let us therefore return to what we said in a previous chapter: What if this day is your last? What if tomorrow morning

28 First troparion of Matins, Great and Holy Monday.

is your last chance to pray and repent and prepare your soul for death? When we perceive our sins and remember our coming judgment, when we become sensitive to the presence of God, we are snapped out of our slumber and we become alert. Do you see now why remembrance of death is so important in spiritual life? Remembrance of death leads to alertness, alertness fosters prayer, and prayer prepares us to meet God.

Step 21

Fear

Fear is danger tasted in advance, a quiver as the heart takes fright before unnamed calamity. Fear is loss of assurance.

A wise priest once said to me, "Don't put fear on the throne." He always spoke in riddles, and it often took me years to realize what he meant by one thing or another. I think in this case, he was exhorting me not to let fear be the motivation for my actions or, more importantly, for my inaction. When we live in fear, we never take risks; we live in a timid fashion, refusing to leave our comfort zone, never able to fully trust in God's care for us.

Fear is, of course, natural, but it must be controlled. To be dominated by fear is a sign of lack of faith and trust in God. Of course, there are irrational fears (phobias) of specific things. I cannot say whether such phobias are related to lack of faith, or whether they can be overcome by faith alone. But fear in general can be a very destructive and oppressive force in one's life. It can dictate our actions and our decisions, and thus may govern our very lives. There are people who think Christianity is all about living in fear, but on the contrary, Christians are called to live a fearless life. There is one exception: Christians fear God. **The servant of the Lord will be afraid only of his Master.**

But the fear of God is not a paralyzing or timid fear. On the contrary, fear of God pushes us to do good, to repent and become more like Christ. This kind of positive fear is aptly expounded in the second-century Christian work, *The Shepherd of Hermas*:

> "Fear," said he, "the Lord, and keep His commandments. For if you keep the commandments of God, you will be powerful in every action, and every one of your actions will be incomparable. For, fearing the Lord, you will do all things well. This is the fear which you ought to have, that you may be saved. But fear not the devil; for, fearing the Lord, you will have dominion over the devil, for there is no power in him. . . . For fears are of two kinds: for if you do not wish to do that which is evil, fear the Lord, and you will not do it; but, again, if you wish to do that which is good, fear the Lord, and you will do it. Wherefore the fear of the Lord is strong, and great, and glorious. Fear, then, the Lord, and you will live to Him, and as many as fear Him and keep His commandments will live to God."[29]

Unfortunately, in contrast to the teaching of Hermas, there are many Orthodox Christians who live in fear of the devil, demons, magic, and curses. This displays a terrible lack of faith.

29 Book Two, Seventh Commandment (Robert-Donaldson translation), http://www.earlychristianwritings.com/text/shepherd.html (accessed on 12/19/12).

Such fear is **contrary to God's providence . . . contrary to spiritual knowledge.** The teaching of Hermas is echoed by many other Fathers: the demons have no power! They can only tempt and frighten, and have no power other than what God permits. This is made abundantly clear in the many accounts of exorcism in the Gospels. The demons fear Christ. They also fear the saints. They should also fear us, rather than us fearing them. There is no dualism in Christianity; God and the devil are not two equal powers playing with humanity like pawns in a chess game. Fear God, and the devil will fear you! This is aptly expressed by St. Nicodemos the Hagiorite:

> Why do you fear the Devil, O Christians? He cannot force you to do anything. The Devil should, rather, fear you, not you the Devil, for you are clad in the armor and panoply of God; you have as a sling the sign of the Precious Cross, with which, and from a distance, you can smite all of the demons; you wield, as a two-edged sword, the Name of our Lord Jesus Christ, which the demons fear and at which they tremble. As for you, if you are willing to keep the commandments of the Lord, and to be the true friends and soldiers of the Heavenly King, you will have no need of magic or any other device of the Devil, and you will trample on him with your feet as though he were a beast, a little sparrow, a scorpion, or an ant. "Behold, I give unto you power to tread on serpents and scorpions, and over all the power of the enemy: and nothing shall by any means hurt you." [Luke 10:19] Hence, if you will, the Devil can become so small and lowly that he resembles an infant; and again, if you will, the

Devil can become so mighty against you that he roars like a fearsome lion and seeks to devour you.[30]

Like all passions, the passion of fear cannot be overcome suddenly. The *Ladder* prescribes mourning as the remedy for fear:

> **Just as one morsel will not fill your stomach, so you will not defeat fear in one move. It will fade in proportion to your mourning and the less we mourn the greater will be our cowardice.**

When we cease to mourn for our sins, we forget our salvation. We compensate for this loss of purpose by attaching undue significance to temporal things—things that are fragile and easily taken from us—and so we end up living with a deep-rooted insecurity. The greater our repentance, the less attached to things we become; and the less attached we become, the more fearless we shall be.

By keeping in mind the Last Judgment, we overcome fear with fear: "Do not fear those who kill the body but cannot kill the soul. But rather fear Him who is able to destroy both soul and body in hell" (Matt. 10:28).

30 *Christian Morality* (Belmont, MA: Institute for Byzantine and Modern Greek Studies, 2012), pp. 342–343.

Step 22

Vainglory

Like the sun which shines on all alike, vainglory beams on every occupation. What I mean is this. I fast, and turn vainglorious. I stop fasting so that I will draw no attention to myself, and I become vainglorious over my prudence. I dress well or badly, and am vainglorious in either case. I talk or hold my peace, and each time I am defeated. No matter how I shed this prickly thing, a spike remains to stand up against me.

Most of us are familiar with the notion of seven deadly sins:

1) Gluttony
2) Lust
3) Avarice
4) Despondency (commonly referred to as sloth)
5) Anger
6) Pride
7) Envy

But in much Eastern Christian literature, eight deadly sins, or vices, are mentioned. This list was probably introduced by Evagrius of Pontus:

1) Gluttony
2) Lust
3) Avarice
4) Dejection
5) Despondency (often referred to as *accidie*)
6) Anger
7) Vainglory
8) Pride

It was St. John Cassian who introduced this list of eight vices to the West. Pope Gregory the Great, however, reduced the number to seven by collapsing dejection and despondency into one, amalgamating vainglory with pride, and adding envy.

While St. John of the Ladder frequently refers to eight vices, he also agrees with St. Gregory's view and considers vainglory and pride to be the same sin. Nonetheless he treats them separately in the *Ladder*, for he regards them as two different stages of the same passion:

> **Vainglory, fully grown, can give birth to pride, which is the beginning and the end of all evil.**

Vainglory, being the beginning of pride, is a spiritual sin. As such, it easily works its way into the very fabric of spiritual life.

Christians are apt to make pious excuses to justify this passion and to fool themselves into thinking they are acting in the name of God rather than for vainglory. As St. John points out:

> **Dread vainglory urges us to pretend that we have some virtue which does not belong to us. It encourages us with the text: "Let your light so shine before men that they will see your good deeds" (Matt. 5:16).**

Furthermore, we seek to disguise our sins in order that people will think us righteous, but our excuse is that we must not scandalize our brethren:

> **Do not conceal your sin because of the idea that you must not scandalize your neighbor. Of course this injunction must not be adhered to blindly. It will depend on the nature of one's sinfulness.**

The notion of Christians being scandalized by the sins of others irks me a great deal. To be "scandalized" is in fact nothing more than a euphemism for being judgmental. Why should anyone be scandalized by the sins of their fellow Christians? Do we so easily forget that we too are sinners? The only sins that should scandalize us are our own!

Yet, as St. John points out, we must have discernment in this matter. We should bear in mind that those who are scandalized are weak Christians. However harsh and judgmental they may seem to be, we should condescend and be understanding of their weakness, just as they should condescend and be compassionate toward those who are guilty of sins of a different nature. As St. Paul writes:

> "We then who are strong ought to bear with the scruples of the weak, and not to please ourselves." (Rom. 15:1)

> "Bear one another's burdens, and so fulfill the law of Christ. For if anyone thinks himself to be something, when he is nothing, he deceives himself. But let each one examine his own work, and then he will have rejoicing in himself alone, and not in another. For each one shall bear his own load." (Gal. 6:2–5)

The greatest example of Christians who are free of vainglory are the saints known as *fools for Christ*. These are rare and remarkable saints. They did not wish to be deemed holy, but instead opted to be condemned as unrighteous. They did not seem to care much about scandalizing their brethren. They broke the mold, overturning the stereotype of saints and the conventions of society, especially religious society. They did not care for social decorum or politeness. They concealed their asceticism, trying to give the impression that they did not observe the fasts of the Church and that they were hypocrites. St. John, in his chapter on discernment, gives us a little example of such behavior:

> **A brother once suffered a disgrace but in his heart he was untroubled by it and in his mind he was prayerful. However, he lamented aloud and by feigned passion hid his dispassion. Another pretended to be eager for the job of father superior when in fact he had no wish at all for it.**

And how am I to speak of the chastity of the brother who entered a brothel for what appeared as a determination to commit sin, and who actually enticed the harlot to take up the ascetic life?[31]

These saints were truly as free of vainglory as anyone could possibly imagine! Criticism did not phase them in the slightest, and they fled flattery and compliments like the plague. For vainglory is, as St. John writes, **a taking note of criticism**, while **it is a great achievement to shrug the praise of men off one's shoulders. . . . Men of high spirit endure offense nobly and willingly. But only the holy and saintly can pass unscathed through praise.**

Notwithstanding the above, once again we must exercise discernment in this matter. I have known people who refuse to compliment others for the sake of their humility, for fear that they will get big-headed, but they do not exercise as much discretion when it comes to criticism. But criticism can be just as harmful to someone who has not already attained great humility. As St. John remarks: **Vainglory induces pride in the favored and resentment in those who are slighted.** If we always held back on complimenting people but never on criticizing them, we would be creating a very grim world indeed! Just about everyone is vainglorious and prideful to some degree, and we must acknowledge that imperfection in others as well as ourselves. It is far from helpful to assume that everyone should deal with criticism like

31 St. Serapion the Sindonite (see F. Nau, "Histoire de Thais," Annale du Musee Guimet vol. xxx, p. 51).

a saint, when the reality is they are far from attaining the virtue of humility.

We said already that vainglory is to be found not only in the ungodly, but also in the most devout Christians. Sometimes there is no difference between the two. Many of us Christians want exactly the same kind of admiration others desire. But in the most devout we find the worst kind of vainglory: a desire to be admired for our piety. This is where vainglory becomes so tragically deep that we are in danger of rendering repentance nearly impossible. For even what we think of as our repentance is in fact vainglory. Thus we end up living one life in private and another life in public, for our faith is in fact nothing more than a show.

The difference between a vainglorious religious person and any other vainglorious person is simply one of taste. One person seeks to be admired for the clothes he is wearing; another seeks the same admiration in priestly vestments. One wishes to be admired for singing on stage, another for chanting in church. One wants to be thought of as tough and cool, another as prayerful and humble. It is the same vainglory in them all.

But the religious kind of vainglory is worse because it passes itself off as religious devotion, as something virtuous. A vainglorious Christian may observe the fasts of the Church when with other Christians, but at home does not observe them at all; he may appear to pray ardently in church, but at home is lazy about prayer. In other words, vainglory is duplicitous. We act one way with one person, another way with another person, and yet another way when alone. Usually it is when we are alone that we are our true selves, but with others we are forever putting on an act. This is why St. John writes that vainglory is **a loss of simplicity and a hypocritical mode of behavior, and the servant of vainglory leads a double life.**

You cannot be saved by pretending to be righteous. You cannot be saved as a pseudo-you. God wants the real you. Better an honest sinner than a fake saint. If we want to become saints, we must offer our true selves, with all our sins and imperfections, to God. But for as long as we are pretending to be saintly, pretending to be someone we are not, there is no possibility of ever becoming who we are meant to be. The saints are those who have become what God wants them to be—the ones whose personalities have been purified through repentance and the shedding of sin. No one who is vainglorious will ever attain sanctity.

Among the saints we find a variety of personalities and ways of life: married and unmarried, martyrs and ascetics, kings and bishops, rich and poor, intellectuals and simpletons. Some were chaste all their lives, others committed many sexual sins; some committed more terrible sins than many of us ever have, yet they became far holier than the most virtuous of us. For every person there is a saint to give us hope, a reminder that sainthood is a real possibility for us too. But for all the variety among the saints, there is one thing that defines every one of them, one thing they all have in common: freedom from vainglory.

Anyone free from this sickness is close to salvation. Anyone affected by it is far removed from the glory of the saints.

Step 23

Pride

Pride begins where vainglory leaves off. Its midpoint comes with the humiliation of our neighbor, the shameless parading of our achievements, complacency, and unwillingness to be found out. It ends with the spurning of God's help, the exalting of one's own efforts and a devilish disposition.

Christian spirituality has always taught that pride is the greatest sin of all. It is very difficult for non-Christians, particularly atheists and humanists, to understand why Christians say this. One can be forgiven for thinking that to call pride the greatest sin is an exaggeration. Surely murder is worse! But when we speak of the passions in Christian spirituality, we are not referring to particular actions (these actions are but the consequences of the passions). Pride cannot be pinpointed in any one particular kind of deed. The reason pride is the greatest sin is that it is in fact the root and cause of so many sorrows and atrocities.

I often hear people say, "I don't need religion to be a good person," but rarely does anyone consider the question, "What does it mean to be a good person?" Usually the response to that question is, "I've never killed anyone; I don't steal." Well, that does not define a good person; it merely describes someone who is not extraordinarily bad. Furthermore, there are saints who have committed those sins, and not only did they not remain wicked, they became holy. So, for Christianity, to be good does not mean never to have done bad things. Rather, it means to come into union with God through repentance. We have to repent to come into union with God because "No one *is* good but One, *that is,* God" (Luke 18:19).

On the other hand, there seems to be a double standard in those who claim that to be good is simply not to do harm to others. For even among the most anti-religious of people, there is no sin that makes a person so unpopular as pride. All the time, I hear people complaining that someone is "full of himself," or that "he thinks the sun shines out of his backside," or something to that effect. It is odd that the very people who reject religion and claim that "it doesn't matter what you believe and do as long as you don't hurt anybody" are the very people you always hear criticizing others for being arrogant or conceited. Since conceit is not actually doing anyone any harm, it is hard to see what the problem is. Haven't these people let the cat out of the bag and shown that they believe in sin and virtue as much as anybody else?

And while they may not be willing to admit it, pride is present in them also. It is present in all of us. The more prideful we are, the more we hate pride in others. The reason for this is simple: Pride is thinking you are better than others or that you deserve better than others. Therefore, when we ourselves are guilty of this or any other sin, we do not recognize it, or at best we justify it; but when we see it in others, we have no mercy at all. Pride is therefore ultimately an opposition to the second great commandment, "You shall love your neighbor as yourself" (Lev. 19:18). For the more we love others as we love ourselves, the less we will be upset that they are better, or better off, than we are.

Yet we still have not reached the ultimate depths of pride. In its purest form, pride is an opposition not only to the second great commandment, but also to the first: "You shall love the LORD your God with all your heart, with all your soul, and with all your strength" (Deut. 6:5). As C. S. Lewis explained:

> In God you come up against something which is in every respect immeasurably superior to yourself. Unless you know God as that—and, therefore, know yourself as nothing in comparison—you do not know God at all.[32]

This is why, according to Christian Tradition, pride was the sin that brought down the devil. Most sins, particularly bodily sins, can often be put down to weakness, to our fallen condition. The devil had no such weakness or condition to contend with. His sin was pure, unadulterated pride. Thus it is the most demonic sin of all.

This is why it easily works its way into the very fabric of spiritual life by wearing the guise of piety. Pride is, ultimately, the worship of our own selves, and so "God" can even become a pious

32 *Mere Christianity* (Harper Collins, 2002), p. 124.

euphemism for the ego. The greatest danger of religious faith is to glorify ourselves in God's name. As St. John puts it:

> **At first it [pride] does not shamelessly urge us to renounce God. I have seen people who speak aloud their thanks to God but who in their hearts are glorifying themselves, something demonstrated by that Pharisee with his "O God, I thank you" (Luke 18:11).**

Religious people are frequently guilty of such a charade. We say, "It's God's will," but what we really mean is, "It's my will." We hear people say things like, "God told me to run for president," "God wants me to be an entrepreneur," "God wants me to be a priest," or some such thing, but what we really mean by "God" is "I." Pride is the deadliest sin because it often disguises itself as faith. And just as the devil was guilty of no other sin but pride, so too pride can condemn a Christian who has committed no other sins. But if pride alone can condemn us, it is possible that humility alone can save us:

> **Pride and nothing else caused an angel to fall from heaven. And so one may reasonably ask whether one may reach heaven by humility alone without the help of any other virtue.**

The idea that pride alone can condemn us to perdition may sound very harsh, even to my fellow Christians. One could be forgiven for thinking that if we are all guilty of pride, there is no hope for any of us. That is, however, a gross oversimplification. If we are capable of acknowledging our pride, if we are capable of seeking forgiveness, of believing we are in need of salvation, then we can be sure that while pride is present in us, it has not completely dominated us. For as long as there is some shred of humility in our hearts, there is hope that we can be saved.

This is why I believe the greatest heresy of all is the belief of some Christians that they are "saved."[33] If we believe we are categorically and without question already saved, it is a good sign that we have been dominated by demonic pride. St. Paul's statement, "If you confess with your mouth the Lord Jesus and believe in your heart that God has raised Him from the dead, you will be saved" (Rom. 10:9), must be read in the context of Christ's words:

> "Not everyone who says to me, 'Lord, Lord,' will enter the kingdom of heaven, but only the one who does the will of my Father who is in heaven. Many will say to Me in that day, 'Lord, Lord, have we not prophesied in Your name, cast out demons in Your name, and done many wonders in Your name?' And then I will declare to them, 'I never knew you; depart from Me, you who practice lawlessness!'" (Matt. 7:21–23)

Faith is not merely "confessional," but relational.

33 The last line of the following chapter of the *Ladder* (Step 24, *On Simplicity*) may seem to contradict this: *If you have the strength to take this step, do not lose heart. For now you are imitating Christ your Master and you have been saved.* But this must be understood within the greater context of the Orthodox understanding of salvation. While we are saved by Christ's Sacrifice, by baptism, and by our repentance, we must never assume that we cannot possibly lose that salvation: *It is as easy for the honest to lapse as it is for evildoers to change their ways.* Salvation is an ongoing process. We are neither "saved" nor "unsaved"; we are "being saved."

I said, as have countless others, that we are all guilty of pride. Unfortunately this can lead us to dismiss pride as something perfectly ordinary and acceptable. Perhaps this is why Christians tend to be more condemning of physical sins (especially sexual sins) than they are of spiritual sins. When it comes to pride, we have a tendency to shrug our shoulders and say, "Everyone is proud. No one is perfect." But we should never be so dismissive of pride.

If we give up striving to attain perfect humility, then we can be sure we have ceased to make any spiritual progress. For pride is not just *a* sin; rather it is, to borrow again the words of C. S. Lewis, "the complete anti-God state of mind."[34] It is, in a sense, *the* sin that separates us from God. **Men can heal the lustful. Angels can heal the malicious. Only God can heal the proud.** All other sins can be repented of if we have enough humility to be contrite, and through that humility alone, we can be saved. As St. Peter of Damascus once wrote:

> If repentance is too much for you, and you sin out of habit even when you do not want to, show humility like the publican (cf. Luke 18:3): this is enough to ensure your salvation.[35]
>
> It is always possible to make a new start by means of repentance. "You fell," it is written, "now arise" (cf. Prov. 24:16). And if you fall again, then rise again, without despairing at all of your salvation, no matter what happens. So long as

34 *Mere Christianity, op. cit.*, p. 122.
35 *Philokalia, op. cit.*, vol. 3, p. 160.

you do not surrender yourself willingly to the enemy, your patient endurance, combined with self-reproach, will suffice for your salvation.[36]

Pride, however, being the opposite of humility, can render salvation impossible, whatever other virtues we may possess. This is why it is so important to acknowledge our pride, to have enough humility to fight it, and to struggle to acquire greater humility. By contrast, the surest way to know that we are full of pride is to think that we are free of it:

> **An old man, very experienced in these matters, once spiritually admonished a proud brother who said in his blindness: "Forgive me, father, but I am not proud." "My son," said the wise old man, "what better proof of your pride could you have given than to claim that you were not proud?"**

Blasphemy and Blasphemous Thoughts

We said earlier that pride, in its purest form, is a rejection of God. It is for this reason that St. John ends his chapter on pride with a section on blasphemy and blasphemous thoughts. Blasphemy is to speak, think, or act in a derogatory way about God or things divine. Thus blasphemy is the outcome of the deepest demonic pride:

> **Blaspheming words rise up in the hearts of the proud . . . unspeakable blasphemy is the child of dreadful pride.**

36 *Philokalia, op. cit.*, p. 170.

Nonetheless, St. John goes on to speak of blasphemous thoughts not only as the fruit of pride, but also as a demonic temptation that even the most righteous can experience. I am not aware of ever having experienced the kind of blasphemous thoughts St. John describes, but I have known others who have experienced them, especially during the Divine Liturgy. From what I have learned of their experiences, they are almost identical to the descriptions contained in the *Ladder*, and it is clear that those who experience such thoughts should ignore them and not think themselves at fault for experiencing them:

> This atrocious foe [the demon of blasphemy] has the habit of appearing during the holy services and even at the awesome hour of the Mysteries [the Eucharist], and blaspheming the Lord and the consecrated elements [the Body and Blood of Christ], showing that these unspeakable, unacceptable, and unthinkable words are not ours but rather those of the God-hating demon. . . . It must be so, for if these dreadful and unholy words are my own, how could I offer humble worship after having partaken of the sacred gift? How could I revile and praise at the same time?
>
> This unholy demon not only blasphemes God and everything that is divine. It stirs up the dirtiest and most obscene thoughts within us, thereby trying to force us to give up praying or to fall into despair. It stops the prayer of many and turns many away from the holy Mysteries . . . but, if we continue to pray to the end, they will retreat, for they do not struggle against those who resist them.

> **If you have blasphemous thoughts, do not think that you are to blame. God knows what is in our hearts and He knows that ideas of this kind come not from us but from our enemies . . . thoughts of this type . . . are caused by that unclean devil. . . . So let us make light of him and pay no regard whatever to his promptings. Let us say: "Get behind me, Satan! I will worship the Lord my God and serve only Him." (Matt. 4:10)**

These temptations are clearly an attempt to make us stop praying, question our own faith, and despair. The only way to fight them is to keep on praying and struggling against pride, which is the root of blasphemy:

> **Let us refrain from passing judgment or condemnation on our neighbor. If we do, then we will not be terrorized by blasphemous thoughts, since the one produces the other.**
>
> **He who has defeated this vice has banished pride.**

Part VI

The Higher Virtues

Step 24

Meekness/Simplicity

Meekness is a mind consistent amid honor or dishonor. Meekness prays quietly and sincerely for a neighbor however troublesome he may be. Meekness is a rock looking out over the sea of anger which breaks the waves which come crashing on it and stays entirely unmoved. Meekness is the bulwark of patience, the door, indeed the mother of love, and the foundation of discernment. . . . It is meekness that earns pardon for our sins, gives confidence to our prayers and makes a place for the Holy Spirit.

In chapter eight, we examined the virtue of meekness in its early stage: freedom from anger. Now the *Ladder* leads us to the higher level of meekness: simplicity, which is the first fruit of an even greater virtue: **Meekness is the precursor of all humility. . . . Before gazing at the sun of humility we must let the light of meekness flow over us.**

The highest form of meekness is the fruit of obedience and freedom from anger. Thus it is the enemy of anger and the spirit of true leadership, an imitation of Christ and the virtue that makes our hearts receptive to the Holy Spirit:

> **Meekness works alongside obedience, guides a religious community, checks frenzy, curbs anger. It is a minister of joy, an imitation of Christ, the possession of angels, a shackle for demons, a shield against bitterness. The Lord finds rest in the hearts of the meek, while the turbulent spirit is the home of the devil.**

Many think of simplicity as simple-mindedness and ignorance, but this is not what it means. Learning and education are not to be shunned. The intellect is not an enemy of faith. While it is certainly true that these things are not necessary for one to acquire virtue, it must be said that for someone who has been endowed with intelligence and a capacity for learning, it is wrong to spurn this gift, as though God wanted only our hearts and not our minds also. As C. S. Lewis put it, "God is no fonder of intellectual slackers than of any other slackers."[37] It is true that clever people are usually more prone to self-conceit than are simple folk, but there are many saints who were highly educated but, notwithstanding their remarkable intellect, acquired the virtue of simplicity. Furthermore, simple people can be just as proud as clever people:

> **If knowledge can cause most people to become vain, perhaps ignorance and lack of learning can make them humble. Yet now and again you find men who pride themselves on their ignorance.**

37 *Mere Christianity, op. cit.*, p. 78.

The virtue of simplicity is not measured by one's IQ, education, or intellectual potential. Simplicity is guilelessness, honesty, integrity. Often simple-minded people are more advanced in this virtue than others because they have the gift of single-mindedness: instead of sitting there thinking things over, they simply focus all their attention on one simple thing and go for it. Perhaps this is why our Lord said, "I thank You, Father, Lord of heaven and earth, that You have hidden these things from *the* wise and prudent and have revealed them to babes" (Matt. 11:25).

One could say that spiritual simplicity is a one-track mind. That may sound negative to many, but what I mean by this is that it is the virtue by which we have shut out all evil thoughts and desires in a single-minded pursuit of union with God:

> **Simplicity is an enduring habit within a soul that has grown impervious to evil thoughts.**

A wonderful example of simplicity is St. Anthony the Great. He was an illiterate peasant, but that kind of simplicity does not concern us here. Intellectual simplicity is neither a vice nor a virtue. It is his spiritual simplicity that is an example to us.

The first time St. Anthony ever heard the gospel was in church. The reading was the conversation between Christ and the rich young ruler (Matt. 19:16–26), in which the young man asks Christ what he must do to gain eternal life. Christ tells him, "If you want to be perfect, go, sell what you have and give to the poor, and you will have treasure in heaven; and come, follow

Me" (Matt. 19:21). With his heart set on fire by that simple command, St. Anthony obeyed, abandoned everything, and retreated into the wilderness to become a monk. He did not think it over; he did not seek an allegorical meaning in the reading; he did not consider how this could apply to him. Instead, he heard Christ commanding him personally, and immediately he obeyed. This is the kind of simplicity St. John is referring to in the *Ladder*.

Simplicity is a childlike innocence. It is **the first characteristic of childhood**: "Be simple and guileless, and you will be as the children who know not the wickedness that ruins the life of men."[38]

When we speak of such innocence, we are not speaking of ignorance or naivety, but of purity of heart. Christ told us to "be wise as serpents and harmless as doves" (Matt. 10:16). Christianity does not require us to be naïve, immature fools. A child's heart does not mean a child's mind.

Why does God want us to be simple? Because He wants us to know Him, and God Himself is simple. Simplicity is the opposite of duplicity and hypocrisy. A double-minded person changes his mind all the time, but "God *is* not a man, that He should lie, nor a son of man, that He should repent [i.e., change His mind]. Has He said, and will He not do? Or has He spoken, and will He not make it good?" (Num. 23:19). Thus simplicity makes us true disciples and imitators of Christ:

38 *The Shepherd of Hermas*, Book Two, Second Commandment (Robert-Donaldson translation), http://www.earlychristianwritings.com/text/shepherd.html (accessed on 3/4/13).

If you wish to draw the Lord to you, approach Him as disciples to a master, in all simplicity, openly, honestly, without duplicity, without idle curiosity. He is simple and uncompounded. And He wants the souls that come to Him to be simple and pure. Indeed you will never see simplicity separated from humility.

If you have the strength to take this step, do not lose heart. For now you are imitating Christ your Master and you have been saved.

Step 25

Humility

> **Humility is constant forgetfulness of one's achievements . . . the admission that in all the world one is the least important and is also the greatest sinner. . . . It is the mind's awareness that one is weak and helpless. . . . It is to forestall one's neighbor at a contentious moment and to be the first to end a quarrel . . . the acknowledgment of divine grace and divine mercy . . . the disposition of a contrite soul and the abdication of one's will. . . . Humility is a grace in the soul and with a name known only to those who have had experience of it.**

If pride is the sin that blinds us to reality, the passion that makes us think ourselves better than we really are, then humility is the virtue by which we see the truth. But if this is so, how is it that the saints never recognize their saintliness? Simply put: they see themselves in comparison to God. The sinfulness they see in themselves *is* the truth, because before God, who is infinitely holy, infinitely perfect, they cannot escape the reality of their unholiness and imperfection. Yet their response to this sense of unworthiness is not one-sided. Along with their repentance and contrition there is indescribable joy, peace, gentleness, and love.

Since it is so difficult for us who lack humility to comprehend it, let us try to think of it in a way we may be able to better identify with. Imagine that a poor, ugly, stupid, unpleasant woman with no prospects of marriage falls in love with the man of her dreams; he is handsome, intelligent, wealthy, noble, and virtuous. Now imagine that her love for this perfect man is requited! Moreover, despite all the wrongs she has committed, and however many times she is unfaithful to him, he never ceases to love and forgive her.

That is how Christ loves us. He is the Bridegroom of the Church, and we are His bride. This bride (the Church) was once a prostitute, a lowly, contemptible, and unclean woman. But the Bridegroom nonetheless loved her so that He took her for His bride and made her not only a decent woman, but a queen. As St. John Chrysostom writes:

> Since Christ came to the Church's place of lodging and found her unclean, filled with impurity, naked and defiled with blood, He bathed her, He polished her, He nourished her and He clothed her with such a garment that it is impossible to find another one better. Christ Himself is the Church's garment. Since He received her in marriage, He raises her up and guides her according to this way. The inheritance has been prepared for the Church.[39]

39 *In Cap. XXIX Genes.*, Hom. LVI, 54:487. Quoted in *The Church's Identity Established Through Images According to Saint John Chrysostom,*

Should such a bride not be eternally grateful for such love and acceptance? In the same way, when I remember that God has taken me, a sinner, and offered me an eternal life of holiness with Him, despite how unworthy I am of such dignity, should I not be moved to tears by such love? And if I am moved to tears, it is because I acknowledge that I am what I am only because of His love, compassion, and holiness, and not by any virtue of my own.

This is one way of understanding humility—that continuous paradox of contrition and joy, the mingling of tears and gratitude. This is why humility overcomes all the passions. Anger, avarice, lust, greed, despondency, hatred, the remembrance of wrongs—all these spring from a deep-seated ingratitude and a blinding love of self. To be humble, on the other hand, is to live in a joyful and peaceful state of thankfulness.

Being the virtue that overwhelms our ego, dissatisfaction, and ingratitude, humility dispels all vainglorious pursuits, all anger and resentment:

> **As soon as the cluster of holy humility begins to flower within us, we come, after hard work, to hate all earthly praise and glory. We rid ourselves of rage and fury; and the more this queen of virtues spreads within our souls through spiritual growth, the more we begin to regard all our good deeds as of no consequence. . . . Where there is humility there will be no sign of hatred, no species of quarrelsomeness, no whiff of disobedience—unless of course some question of faith arises.**

Protopresbyter Gus George Christo (Orthodox Research Institute, 2006), p. 162.

Here St. John reminds us that obedience (which is part and parcel of humility) is not blind subjugation. When obedience means betraying our faith, doing or agreeing to something we know to be wrong, humility does not compel us to obey, but rather gives us the courage to take a stand. For humility is rooted not in cowardice, but in the fear and love of God.

We Christians are always bleating on about humility, yet hardly any of us have it. Perhaps we forget that humility is not merely a virtue to be admired, but one to be strived for. It is all very well praising saints and spiritual fathers for their great humility, but unless we make some effort to acquire humility ourselves, such praise will not get us very far. As St. John writes:

> **There is a difference between being humble, striving for humility, and praising the humble.**

We are tempted to be passive about the virtues. We think of faith, humility, patience, self-control, and all other virtues as nothing more than divine gifts—you have them or you don't. But then there would be no sense in God commanding us to have faith, to be patient, to pray, to forgive. We are all capable of growing in virtue just as we are all capable of falling into sin.

While it is true that God does not give spiritual gifts in equal measure (as we see in the Parable of the Talents in Matt. 25:14–30), it is clear that we will have to account for what we have done with the gifts God has given us. A person of meager virtue who has strived harder than another who possesses greater virtue may be the more virtuous in God's eyes, simply because his virtue was acquired by working for his salvation with the little he had, while the other has complacently relied on God's gifts:

> **Whoever is eager for the peaceful haven of humility will never cease to do all that he can to get there.**

We said before that the humble are always ignorant of their humility. In the same way, the repentant are always ignorant of their repentance, for only the humble can repent. So we have in the spiritual life a certain paradox: we cannot acquire virtue without repentance, but we cannot repent without virtue. St. John explains this with a brief story about a certain monk:

> **The monk got up and on the wall of his cell he wrote in sequence the names of the major virtues: perfect love, angelic humility, pure prayer, unassailable chastity, and others of a similar kind. The result was that whenever vainglorious thoughts began to puff him up, he would say: "Come! Let us go to be judged." Going to the wall he read the names there and would cry out to himself: "When you have every one of these virtues within you, then you will have an accurate sense of how far from God you still are."**

So how can we acquire humility? St. John tells us the answer is different for each person:

> **Some drive out empty pride by thinking to the end of their past misdeeds, for which they were forgiven and which now serve as a spur to humility. Others, remembering the passion of Christ, think of themselves as eternally in debt. Others hold themselves in contempt when they think**

of their daily lapses. Others come to possess the mother of graces by way of their continuous temptations, weaknesses, and sins.

The above passage may sound morbid to many, but on the flipside of humble repentance there is hope:

Contrition is the outcome of a lapse. A man who has lapsed breaks down and prays without arrogance, though with laudable persistence, disarrayed and yet clinging to the staff of hope, indeed using it to drive off the dog of despair.

We also said previously that humility is the outcome of gratitude. St. John takes this idea further. He reminds us that when we are truly humble and grateful, we pray for little. We do not think of ourselves as deserving of anything, and this means our prayer is not about asking for things. Instead we pray only for God's mercy, forgiveness, and holiness:

The man who asks God for less than he deserves will certainly receive more, as is shown by the publican who begged forgiveness but obtained salvation (cf. Luke 18:10–14). And the robber asked only to be remembered in the kingdom, yet he inherited all of Paradise (cf. Luke 23:43).

This is why, in the services of the Church, our prayers are always simple, modest, and spiritual in nature: we ask for mercy, forgiveness, guidance, deliverance, and salvation. We do not ask for wealth, success, the fulfillment of our wishes and ambitions. If we pray for the latter things, we are not really praying at all, at least not to the true God. Instead we are praying to the god of our imagination and ego—the god who gives me exactly what I want, or may give me what I want if I do certain things to appease him. Those who truly know God do not pray that way.

Humility is not merely one of the virtues—it is the virtue that makes all others possible and that purifies our wills and motives. People may do good things but for the wrong reasons. We see this spelled out clearly in the Gospels, where Christ says of the Pharisees: "All their works they do to be seen by men" (Matt. 23:5). And our Lord exhorts us to be sure that our actions are inspired by good motives and not vainglory:

> "Take heed that you do not do your charitable deeds before men, to be seen by them. Otherwise you have no reward from your Father in heaven. Therefore, when you do a charitable deed, do not sound a trumpet before you as the hypocrites do in the synagogues and in the streets, that they may have glory from men. Assuredly, I say to you, they have their reward. But when you do a charitable deed, do not let your left hand know what your right hand is doing, that your charitable deed may be in secret; and your Father who sees in secret will Himself reward you openly. . . .
>
> "Moreover, when you fast, do not be like the hypocrites, with a sad countenance. For they disfigure their faces that they may appear to men to be fasting. Assuredly, I say to you, they have their reward. But you, when you fast, anoint your head and wash your face, so that you do not appear to men to be fasting, but to your Father who *is* in the secret place; and your Father who sees in secret will reward you openly." (Matt. 6:1–4, 16–18)

Pride poisons even good actions. Thus St. John writes: **Where there is no humility, all is rotten.**

But if it is indeed the case that good deeds are spoiled by conceited motives, could it be possible that humility can sanctify even our errors? It is said that "the path to hell is paved with good intentions." I wonder if the opposite is true: it is the path to heaven that is paved with good intentions.

> **Every act that is not the product of personal inclination or of impurity will be imputed to us for good, especially if done for the sake of God and not for someone else. This is so, even if the actions themselves are not completely good.**

We have already heard St. John pose the question **whether one may reach heaven by humility alone without the help of any other virtue.** Now he dares to answer that question:

> **If pride turned some of the angels into demons, then humility can doubtless make angels out of demons. So take heart, all you sinners.**

In a previous chapter, we were told: **As for humility, ask in due time who it is that bore her.** So we cannot leave this chapter until we have asked that question. The answer humility gives is rather cryptic:

> **"Why are you in such a rush to learn the name of my begetter? He has no name, nor will I reveal him to you until you have God for your possession."**

The answer is reminiscent of the answer the Lord gave to Jacob and Manoah when they asked for His name: "Why *is* it *that* you ask about My name?" (Gen. 32:29); "Why do you ask My name, seeing it *is* wonderful?" (Judges 13:18). And we cannot forget the Lord's answer to Moses on Mount Sinai when he asked the same question: "I AM WHO I AM"[40] (Ex. 3:14).

This suggests that the answer to the question, "Who, or what, begets humility?" is God Himself.

40 In the Ancient Greek version of the Old Testament (the Septuagint), which is that of the Orthodox Church, the Lord replies, "I am the one who is," or, "I am the living one."

Step 26

Discernment

Among beginners, discernment is real self-knowledge; among those midway along the road to perfection, it is a spiritual capacity to distinguish unfailingly between what is truly good and what in nature is opposed to the good; among the perfect, it is a knowledge resulting from divine illumination, which with its lamp can light up what is dark in others . . . discernment is . . . a solid understanding of the will of God in all times, in all places, in all things . . . an uncorrupted conscience . . . pure perception.

You may have noticed by now that the steps of the *Ladder* are not independent of one another. The passions and virtues are not to be understood in isolation as distinct steps. We may have made a beginning of various virtues, but we have yet to make any advanced progress in them, and so many passions continue to dominate us in spite of our little spiritual development. To reach the heights of spirituality, we must keep battling on in every aspect of Christian life. One virtue alone may be able to save us, but only all of them combined can lead us to holiness and the likeness of God. In a similar way, true discernment requires mastery over all the passions, but that is not to say we may not all be able to make a little progress in it.

The above passage points out three stages of discernment. The beginning is self-knowledge. The intermediate stage is to be able to distinguish between what is truly good and bad. The advanced stage is divine illumination, by which we are able to perceive God's will. Let us examine the virtue of discernment in these three stages.

Stage 1—Self-Knowledge

To "know thyself" is the first level of discernment. When we begin spiritual life, enthusiasm must be tempered with knowledge and humility, or we will try to go too far too fast. At the same time, we must not allow our own weakness and reluctance to change our ways to dictate our spiritual life and thus cause us to remain content with our failure to reach the Christian ideal, confusing "difficult" with "impossible." We are only called to do what we can, but many people interpret that as doing what we want or what makes us comfortable. To live the gospel is not easy, but neither is it impossible. The commandments to love your enemy, to forsake all for the gospel, to endure affliction and turn the other cheek are not for the select few, but for every one of us:

> **No one should plead inability to do what is asked of us in the gospels, since there are souls who have accomplished far more than is commanded.**

> Evil or passion is not something naturally implanted in things. God is not the creator of passions. On the other hand, there are many natural virtues that have come to us from Him. These clearly include the following: mercy, something even the pagans have; love, for even dumb animals bewail the loss of one of their own; faith, which all of us can generate of ourselves; hope, since we all lend, and take to the sea, and sow seed, expecting to do well out of it. Hence if love comes naturally to us—and it has been shown to be so—if it is the bond and the fulfillment of the law, virtues cannot be too far from nature. For which reason, those who claim to be unable to practice the virtues should be ashamed of themselves.

Unfortunately, because God's commandments are not easy to keep (due to our own sins and weaknesses), we are apt to dismiss them as unrealistic and idealistic. We also tend to think of them as negative burdens rather than as positive opportunities. Thus we make a mockery of God, who gave us these commandments. While some Christians like to take so many passages of Scripture literally and use such passages against others when it suits them, when it comes to the things they are not so keen on doing themselves, such as forgiving enemies, they come up with a list of excuses as long as your arm. It is therefore essential that we have the humility to acknowledge that we keep falling short of God's commandments, and that we need to repent.

Nonetheless, we must be mindful of our limitations. Some strive to pray and fast beyond their ability, which often leads them to giving up and losing hope. Being too austere can be just as detrimental to our spiritual life as being too lax:

> **There are brave souls who lovingly and humbly undertake tasks that are well beyond them. There are proud hearts that do the same. Now it often happens that our enemies[41] deliberately inspire us to do things beyond our capacities, and their objective is to make us falter so that we abandon even what lies within our power, and make ourselves ridiculous to our enemies.**

This is why we ought to have a spiritual father who will help us discern what we personally should do to progress in our spiritual life, and we should humbly accept his counsel and guidance.

Stage 2—Discerning Good and Bad

Everyone is endowed with the ability to discern between good and bad. Sometimes this discernment is distorted by our passions or by mental illness. But the distinction between good and bad can be further distorted by externals. Our perception is limited to what we see, but we do not know what is in a person's soul. The gift of discernment is to acquire the eyes of God, who looks at the inner man: "The LORD does not see as man sees; for man looks at the outward appearance, but the LORD looks at the heart" (1 Kingdoms [1 Samuel] 16:7). Furthermore, we do not see where a person's actions or decisions may lead, but God foresees all things.

41 When St. John speaks of "enemies" in the spiritual life, he is usually referring to the demons.

Our inability to discern accurately is one reason we must never judge others. It is also the reason we must not think "one size fits all" in Christian spirituality. By this I mean that a spiritual father may tell one person to fast rigorously, but not another. The reason is that the spiritual father has discerned what will be helpful or harmful to each person individually. We should therefore not judge someone who fasts less rigorously than we do or prays less than we do, for they may be acting in obedience and with the knowledge that they are working within their limits:

> **One man's medicine can be another man's poison, and something can be a medicine to the same man at one time and a poison at another.**

We forever judge and criticize and accuse, but in so doing we show that we have no discernment. We may accuse others of hypocrisy for not practicing what they preach, but St. John says:

> **Anyone in the grip of previous bad habits and yet still able to give teaching, although only by their words, should do so. . . . Shamed by their own words, they may finally begin to practice what they preach.**
>
> **Do not be a harsh critic of those who resort to eloquence to teach many important things, who have few actions to match their words. For edifying words have often compensated for a lack of deeds. All of us do not get an equal share of every good, and for some the word is mightier than the deed (cf. Ps. 102:20–21; 1 Pet. 5:8) and vice versa for others.**

We may think of someone as a bad person, but we do not consider that if we had been through the same things that he went through, we might be infinitely worse. God, who knows all things, judges us not only by our works, but also by our efforts and intentions; not only by our achievements and successes, but also by our lot in life:

> **God judges us by our intentions, but because of His love for us He only demands from us such actions as lie within our power. Great is the man who does all that lies within his power, but greater still is the man who, in all humility, tries to do more.**
>
> **Sometimes one's upbringing may be responsible for the greatest evils. Sometimes it may be the company we keep. And often it may be the sheer perversity of the soul that produces disaster.**
>
> **The greater our conflicts the greater our rewards. There will be no crown for the man who has never been under attack, and the man who perseveres in spite of any failures will be glorified as a champion by the angels.**
>
> **I have observed men who were sick in soul and body and who, out of a sense of the great number of their sins, tried to do what was beyond their power, and therefore failed. To these I say that God judges our repentance not by our exertions but by our humility.**

As we hear in the beautiful Paschal homily of St. John Chrysostom, God "accepts the work done" but also "welcomes the intention. He honors the achievement; He praises the purpose."[42]

Certainly, those who struggle the most against the passions, even if they fail miserably, will receive an even greater reward than those whose virtues come to them naturally:

> I cannot say why it is that some people appear to be naturally inclined to temperance or silence or purity or modesty or meekness or contrition. Others have to fight hard against their own natures to acquire these, they have to force themselves on to the best of their ability, suffering occasional defeat on the way; and it seems to me that the very fact of having to struggle against their own natures somehow puts them in a higher category than the first kind.

A further difficulty in discerning between good and bad is that sometimes we are faced with a choice between two evils. St. John Climacus confronts this problem in a refreshingly simple, straightforward way:

> Long ago, in my young days, I came to a city or to a village, and while sitting at table I was afflicted at the same time by thoughts of gluttony and of vainglory. Knowing and fearing the outcome of gluttony, I decided to give in to vainglory. I also knew that in the young, the demon of gluttony often overcomes the demon of vainglory. This is not to be wondered at, for among people of the world love of money is the root of all evil, whereas in monks it is gluttony.

42 The Paschal Vigil Service.

> **Again, there are some who infringe a commandment for the sake of a commandment. I have known young men who were bound by ties of honorable affection but who, to avoid any scandal, agreed to avoid each other's company for a time.**

In addition to facing such dilemmas, we often find that our good actions and sentiments are intertwined with bad ones:

> **When we acquire virtues we can sometimes find ourselves involved with the vices which are imperceptibly interwoven with them. . . . Gluttony can be caught up with hospitality; lust with love; cunning with discernment . . . conceit with joy; laziness with hope. . . . And behind all the virtues follows vainglory.**

We would be treading a dangerous path if we chose to abandon all good for fear of sin. Therefore, we must often choose between doing what is right while knowing that our motives may not be entirely pure, and doing no good at all. We should not allow the fear of sin to override the desire for what is good.

So what may seem at first to be a straightforward thing of which we are all capable—to discern between good and bad—is not always so easy. We need the gift of discernment.

Stage 3—Perceiving the Will of God

The final stage of discernment is to be able to perceive God's will for each of us. Of course God's will is made plain to us in the commandments, but the question of how each person can exercise these commandments is not always such a simple matter, nor is it clear how each Christian can commit his life to God. People often find themselves faced with certain dilemmas, such as having to work on Sundays, or having a job in which the work may contradict a person's religious beliefs, and so St. John tells us we should always question whether what we do is in accordance with God's will:

> **Whatever you do, however you live, whether you live under obedience or whether you are independent, in what you do openly or in your spiritual life, let it be your rule and practice to ask if what you do is in accordance with the will of God.**

The first step to discerning whether something is in accordance with God's will is our own conscience:

> **Let our God-directed conscience be our aim and rule in everything.**

Note that St. John uses the term **God-directed conscience.** Even our conscience may not be in accordance with God's will, and so the conscience must be purified if it is to be a true guide for our spiritual life: **Those who wish to discover the will of God must begin by mortifying their own will.**

Given very few of us can really rely on conscience alone to perceive the will of God, what other options are left to us? **We should turn humbly and in confidence to the fathers and we should accept their counsel.** We ought not to rely wholly on our own judgment, but should seek the counsel of others. Even if our spiritual father does not possess the expert discernment of which St. John speaks (and there are very few people who do possess such a level of discernment), **we should nonetheless heed their advice, even when the counsel goes against the grain, even when the advice comes from those who do not seem very spiritual. For God will not lead astray the souls who, trusting and guileless, yield in lowliness to the advice and decision of their neighbor.** Our obedience and humility are more important than the discernment of our advisor:

> **Even if those consulted are stupid, God immaterially and invisibly speaks through them and anyone who faithfully submits to this norm will be filled with humility.**

On Expert Discernment

Discernment is a large part of what I would call "advanced spirituality" (which is no doubt the reason it is the subject of one of the longest chapters in the *Ladder*), and advanced spirituality is not as simple as people like to make out. People often complain that theology is too complicated. "I am not interested in theology, only in spirituality," is something I have often heard Christians say. I find it curious that people consider advanced spirituality any easier to comprehend than advanced theology.

The highest degree of discernment—what St. John calls "expert discernment"—is by no means an easy thing to recognize or comprehend. The reason for this is quite straightforward: the one who possesses expert discernment can, through divine illumination, see into the hearts and minds of others, and so their actions and decisions, being based on a knowledge we do not possess, may seem wrong to many of us. Moreover, a person who possesses expert discernment can perceive God's will in every case. The result of this is that the actions, words, and decisions of such people can seem improper to those who do not know and understand God's will. St. John gives us an example of this:

> **Two monks once developed an unhealthy fondness for one another. But a discerning and very experienced father brought them to the stage of detesting each other. He made them enemies by telling each man he was being slandered by the other, and by this piece of chicanery he warded off the demon's malice, and by causing hatred he brought an end to what was an unclean affection.**

The action of that spiritual father would seem to any sensible Christian a terrible action, a transgression of the commandment not to bear false witness against one's neighbor. Yet because the spiritual father in question had such incredible discernment that he knew this course of action would produce the desired result, it was an act not of malice, envy, or poor judgment, but of love and wisdom. I confess that I too would be critical of such a spiritual father, but that is because I lack discernment, and I could not possibly know that his action was pure and, in that particular situation, the best thing to do.

Few of us can acquire enough discernment to recognize when

someone has discerned correctly. So let us at least take this course of action: let us not judge or become angry when we hear of or witness such things. Rather, let us humbly consider that the action was inspired by good intentions. Whether we recognize that the action was right or go on believing it was wrong, let us at least not condemn. It is not a sin to lack discernment, but it is a sin to pass judgment.

Part VII

Union with God

Step 27

Stillness

Stillness of the body is the accurate knowledge and management of one's feelings and perceptions. Stillness of soul is the accurate knowledge of one's thoughts and is an unassailable mind.

At the Divine Liturgy of St. Basil the Great on Great and Holy Saturday, we chant, "Let all mortal flesh keep silent, and with fear and trembling stand; let us ponder no earthly things . . ."[43]

As we contemplate the profound mystery of the death of God, of Life lying in the tomb, and as we prepare for Holy Communion, we are commanded to acquire inward stillness.

The call to such stillness may be particularly acute on Great Saturday, but it is a state of being all Christians are called to acquire in the presence of God. Those who philosophize about God are full of thoughts and distractions, but those who stand in His presence are silenced. The former consider the theory of God, but the latter know Him personally as Lord, Master, Father, and Friend. It should therefore not take us by surprise that stillness is the calling not only of the

43 The Cherubic Hymn. It is also the Cherubic Hymn of the Liturgy of St. James.

monk and the hermit, but of every Christian, for we are all called to know and love God, and to stand before Him with fear, reverence, and humility.

When someone begins to work toward acquiring inward stillness, he must spend time in solitude, avoiding noisiness and distraction whenever possible. In solitude he seeks union with God through prayer: **Stillness is worshipping God unceasingly and waiting on Him.**

The fruit of many years of true prayer is an inward stillness that is no longer troubled by noisiness and external distractions:

> **The start of stillness is the rejection of all noisiness as something that will trouble the depths of the soul. The final point is when one has no longer a fear of noisy disturbance, when one is immune to it.**

This is, in fact, one of the key principles of monastic solitude: we leave the world not out of hatred for the world, but that we may be able eventually to return to it with perfect love and peacefulness:

> **The solitary runs away from everyone, but does so without hatred, just as another runs toward the crowd, even if without enthusiasm.**

If we seek solitude not because we love prayer and yearn for union with God, but simply because we like to be alone or because people annoy us, then solitude, instead of helping our spiritual life, will hinder it. If we find our passions are not diminished after spending time in solitude, then we are not practicing stillness, only aloneness:

> **The following are signs of stillness practiced wrongly—poverty of spiritual treasures, anger on the increase, a growth of resentment, love diminished, a surge of vanity.**

This is why St. John says **the life of stillness, especially when practiced by solitaries, must be guided by conscience and common sense.**

Before we acquire stillness, crowds and cities can be frustrating and noisy places for us, but whoever acquires perfect stillness can be at peace anywhere:

> **Do not be afraid of loud nonsense. The spirit of mourning is neither afraid of it nor upset by it.**

What Can We Do?

What can we who are not called to a life of solitude do to acquire stillness? There is not one single way for everyone. As St. John writes:

> **Some work to reduce the passions. Others sing psalms and spend most of their time in prayer. Some turn to the depths of contemplation. But whatever the situation is, let it be investigated in accordance with the ladder and accepted in the Lord.**

Some find peace and stillness in reading, others in handiwork or art, yet others in music. While these things may seem to us to be neutral and not specifically spiritual or godly activities, if they help us to acquire some measure of stillness, they should not be dismissed so quickly as spiritually unprofitable.

Another thing we could do is to make time each day to quiet down. Even one or two small pockets of time to retreat into solitude for ten minutes or so can help us enormously. Some are fortunate enough to work near a church, where they can go for about ten minutes during their lunch break. I have known people who benefit a great deal from this opportunity. Others may manage half an hour of solitude at home in their prayer corner or in their study every evening.

But what should we do with those precious few opportunities for solitude? It is not always necessary to speak to God. But often, thoughts and concerns distract our silence. One thing we can do is give a little time to the reading of Scripture. Some like to carry a small pocket Bible or New Testament with them, which they can dip into at opportune moments (on the bus or train, on their lunch break, while in church).

We should read Scripture prayerfully, not inquisitively. There is a time and a place for studying or analyzing Scripture, but for the purpose of acquiring stillness, we should read it as though it is prayer. Indeed, in Orthodox worship, the hearing of the Scriptures is something we pray and prepare for, so before we begin, it is good to say a brief prayer, such as this short extract from a prayer of Vespers:

Blessed are You, O Lord, teach me Your statutes.
Blessed are You, O Master, make me understand Your statutes.
Blessed are You, O Holy One, enlighten me with Your statutes.

We could also adapt for private use the Prayer before the Gospel at the Divine Liturgy, as follows:

Master, Lover of mankind, make the pure light of Your divine knowledge shine in my heart, and open the eyes of my mind to understand the message of Your Gospel. Implant in me the fear of Your blessed commandments, so that, having trampled down all carnal desires, I may pursue a spiritual way of life, thinking and doing all things that are pleasing to You.

We could also do the same with the last prayer of the First Hour:

Christ, the true Light, who enlightens and sanctifies everyone who comes into the world, cause the light of Your countenance to shine upon me, that in it, I may see Your unapproachable Light, and guide my steps to the doing of Your commandments. At the intercessions of the Most-holy Mother of God, and of all Your saints. Amen.

Remember that God is speaking to you, and He is calling you to live, not merely to know, the gospel:

Light and recollection come to the mind by way of reading the Scriptures. The words are those of the Holy Spirit, and they provide guidance to the readers. Let your reading be a preliminary to action, since you are a doer (cf. James 1:22).

Put the words into practice, and then further reading will be unnecessary. Try to be enlightened by the words of salvation through your labors and not from books. And until you have acquired spiritual power, do not read works that have various levels of meaning since, being obscure, they may bring darkness over the weak.

There is something else that has helped many to acquire inner stillness:

Let the remembrance of Jesus be present with your every breath. Then you will appreciate the value of stillness.

Here St. John is probably referring to the practice of the Jesus Prayer. We already touched on this prayer in a previous chapter, and we shall return to it in the following chapter, but I should like to comment further on it now before we leave the subject of stillness.

We said before that the Jesus Prayer, being such a concise prayer, can be constantly repeated inwardly in any situation. The purpose of this practice is to sanctify time and to create inner stillness, as we purify our thoughts and actions with the repeated invocation of the name of Jesus.

The Jesus Prayer has multiple forms. The longest and most common form is, "Lord Jesus Christ, Son of God, have mercy on me, a sinner"; while a shorter invocation, "Lord Jesus Christ, have mercy on me," is also often used. Some find it helpful to use a prayer rope (*komboskini*), much like a rosary, to keep the mind focused on the prayer when it wanders, repeating the prayer as each knot of the rope is passed through the forefinger and thumb.

We should be careful that the prayer rope itself does not become a way of making a show of our prayer (see Matt. 6:5–6). It is best to keep it concealed in our pocket and to use it discreetly when necessary. It is only an aid to prayer, and when you cannot be discreet, your fingers could do just as well as an aid to concentration.

These are a few simple suggestions for how we can acquire a small measure of stillness in the midst of a hectic lifestyle. But be under no illusion that we can acquire perfect stillness by giving such a small amount of time to solitude and prayer. The masters of inward prayer spent years in the crucible of ascesis, giving themselves wholly to supplication, worship, and contemplation for many hours every day. There are no quick and easy paths to perfect stillness. Nonetheless, a little time spent in heartfelt supplication each day will bring us closer to God than many years of empty, insincere prayer. So take heart, for stillness is a real possibility for all of us if we truly love God with all our being.

Few of us will ever attain an unshakeable stillness, but we are all able to have a taste of it, especially when we go to church to worship, and above all when we participate in the Divine Liturgy and receive Christ's Body and Blood in the Eucharist. For nowhere is the presence of God more tangible than in the Divine Liturgy. In the presence of God, we are called to be still that we may hear the Holy Spirit's "still small voice" (3 Kingdoms [1 Kings] 19:12) and learn His will: "Be still, and know that I *am* God" (Ps. 45/46:10).

Step 28

Prayer

> Prayer is by nature a dialog and a union of man with God. Its effect is to hold the world together. It achieves a reconciliation with God. . . . It is an expiation of sin, a bridge across temptation, a bulwark against affliction. . . .
>
> Prayer is future gladness, action without end, wellspring of virtues, source of grace, hidden progress, food for the soul, enlightenment of the mind, an axe against despair, hope demonstrated, sorrow done away with.

For most Christians, prayer is something we do at certain times of day, and it is an important part of Christian life. But for the saints, prayer is not merely a part of life, it *is* their life: it imbues their very being and is present in every action.

Many think of prayer as "speaking to God," but as St. John points out, prayer is not a monologue, but a dialogue.

How to Pray

So how can we learn to converse with God? In other words, how can we learn to pray? This is not a strange question to ask. When Christ's disciples asked Him to "teach us to pray, as John also taught his disciples," He responded thus:

"When you pray, say:
Our Father in heaven,
Hallowed be Your name.
Your kingdom come.
Your will be done
On earth as *it is* in heaven.
Give us day by day our daily bread.
And forgive us our sins,
For we also forgive everyone who is indebted to us.
And do not lead us into temptation,
But deliver us from the evil one." (Luke 11:2-4)

Ever since then, the Lord's Prayer has held a central place in Christian worship. This prayer teaches us to pray not only by giving us words to say, but by showing us how we should approach the act of prayer and what things we should pray for. These elements of prayer are the following:

Praise and adoration:

"Hallowed be Your name."

Hope and expectation:

"Your kingdom come."

The acceptance of God's will and not our own:

"Your will be done
On earth as it is in heaven."

Praying only for our common and immediate needs:

"Give us day by day our daily bread."

Praying for forgiveness and forgiving others in turn:

"And forgive us our sins,
For we also forgive everyone who is indebted to us."

Praying for help in the face of temptation:

"And do not lead us into temptation,
But deliver us from the evil one."

St. John of the Ladder provides us with a similar structure for prayer:

> **Heartfelt thanksgiving should have first place in our book of prayer. Next should be confession and genuine contrition of soul. After that should come our request to the universal King. This method of prayer is best.**

That is a general guideline, but there are many forms of prayer:

> **The attitude of prayer is the same for all, but there are many kinds of prayer and many different prayers. Some talk and deal with God as with a friend and master, lifting their praises and their requests to Him not for themselves but for others. Some look for greater spiritual treasures and glory and for greater assurance in their adversary. Some look for rank and others for relief from their debts. Some seek freedom from jail or for charges against them to be dropped.**[44]

44 Although it is not altogether clear, St. John may be speaking here metaphorically: *greater spiritual treasures and glory* = greater virtue; *greater assurance in their adversary* = deliverance from temptation; *rank* = a greater degree of holiness; *relief from their debts . . . freedom from jail or for charges against them to be dropped* = forgiveness of sins.

The Three Levels of Prayer

One of the greatest teachers of prayer, St. Theophan the Recluse, refers to three stages, or levels, of prayer[45]:

1) Spoken prayer
2) Mental prayer
3) Prayer of the heart

Though these are often referred to as *levels* or *stages*, I prefer to think of them as *forms*. The reason is that though each form is higher than the last, even the lowest form of prayer never disappears from the spiritual life of even the most advanced practitioners of prayer. Let us, then, examine these three forms of prayer.

1. Spoken Prayer

We begin to learn how to pray through the Church—through its prayers, hymns, and services. Since the earliest days of the Church, the psalms have been the backbone of Orthodox prayer and worship. The psalms are therefore a good place to begin learning how to pray. We should remember, however, that the psalms are not only prayers, but prophecies (Psalm 21/22 being an obvious example).

I mention this because there are passages in the psalms in

45 *The Path of Prayer: Four Sermons on Prayer*, trans. Esther Williams (Chicago: Praxis Institute Press, 1992), p. 17.

which we find prayers or expressions of hope that our enemies shall be destroyed, which some Christians may find uncomfortable (e.g., Psalms 9/10:15; 10/11:6; 82/83:9-18; 40/41:10). If we understand that the psalms are not just prayers, but prophecies and works of theology, then we can read them without any sense of our prayer contradicting the commandments to "love your enemies, bless those who curse you, do good to those who hate you, and pray for those who spitefully use you and persecute you" (Matt. 5:44).

The most helpful way to learn to pray through the services of the Church is with a prayer book. Such books give us a structure of prayer (morning and evening prayers, prayers before and after meals, and so on). These prayers are often used in common worship (for example, the Hours, Small Compline, Vespers), and so even when we are alone, we are conscious of praying as members of the church community. They include prayers to the Holy Trinity. We address Christ as God, and we have supplications to the Mother of God and the saints in which we ask them to intercede to Christ for us. Thus we learn to pray through the Church's worship and theology.

Praying through prayer books is not the only form of spoken prayer. While these help us to pray correctly, that is, in an Orthodox way, we often find that our prayer can be dry: we end up reciting prayers without meaning them or understanding them. Certainly, we should persist in saying these prayers. For the more accustomed we grow to using them, the easier it will be for these prayers to become our own and to be carried into the second stage of prayer: mental prayer.

But in addition to using set prayers, we can pray in our own words. Such prayer is by no means unacceptable. On the contrary, our own words can be the most powerful prayers of all:

> **Pray in all simplicity. The publican and the prodigal son were reconciled to God by a single utterance. . . . In your prayers there is no need for high-flown words, for it is the simple and unsophisticated babblings of children that have more often won the heart of the Father in heaven. . . . Try not to talk excessively in your prayer, in case your mind is distracted by the search for words. One word from the publican sufficed to placate God, and a single utterance saved the thief. Talkative prayer frequently distracts the mind and deludes it, whereas brevity makes for concentration.**

Our prayers should be simple. Christ Himself warns us about verbosity and saying too much in prayer:

> "When you pray, do not use vain repetitions as the heathen *do*. For they think that they will be heard for their many words. Therefore do not be like them. For your Father knows the things you have need of before you ask Him." (Matt. 6:7-8)[46]

46 People sometimes accuse the Orthodox of using "vain repetitions" in prayer when they hear us repeating "Lord, have mercy" over and over again. The Greek word for "vain repetitions" is βαττολογια, which is like "babbling" or "waffling." When we read Christ's injunction to avoid vain repetitions in context, "they think that they will be heard for their many words . . . do not be like them. For your Father knows the things you

Notwithstanding the above, it is not easy to spend more than a few moments in prayer with limited words, and so when we are making a beginning of prayer, we should not restrict ourselves to praying spontaneously; we should also read the established prayers of the Church. As St. John writes:

> **"I would prefer to speak five words with my understanding" (1 Cor. 14:19) and so on, says the mighty practitioner of great and high prayer. But prayer of this sort is foreign to infant souls, and so because of our imperfection we need quantity as well as quality in the words of our prayer, the former making a way for the latter.**

The most obvious case of spontaneous prayer is praying for others. This is not only an act of prayer, but an act of love. There is a wonderful story about the power not only of faith, but also of love, in prayer:

> Two men found themselves stranded on a remote island. They both decided to dedicate themselves to prayer, each taking a different part of the island. Everything the first man prayed for was granted to him: food, drink, warmth, shelter; but the other man had nothing.
>
> Eventually, the first man prayed for rescue, and sure enough, a boat came to take him away. As he boarded the

---

have need of before you ask Him," we must conclude that the meaning of βαττολογια is something between verbosity and asking for many things. If this is the case, then the repetitions we find in Orthodox prayer and worship are not at all vain, but are, in fact, a remedy to the very thing Christ is denouncing. We keep our minds focused on "the one thing needful" (see Luke 10:42)—which is God's mercy—rather than our own desires.

boat, he heard God calling to him: “Why are you leaving your brother behind on the island?”

The man said, “He does not deserve to be rescued, since none of his prayers were answered.”

“You are mistaken,” the Lord replied, “He had but one prayer, which I did answer. Were it not for that, you would have received nothing.”

“Tell me,” the man said, “what did he pray for, that I should owe him anything?”

The Lord replied, “He prayed that all your prayers be answered.”

When we are still learning to pray, we may end up asking for the wrong things. We allow our passions to dictate the petitions we make to God. So it is no wonder that our prayers are not always answered! But praying for others—even if we are praying for something we think is best for that person, when God knows it is not—is unselfish. We think of charity as being something that concerns only material things—giving food or money to the needy—but prayer itself is an act of charity: we give up some of our time to dedicate to praying for others. Even if we are not experts in prayer and possess a weak faith, we should not refuse to pray for others, nor should we think our faith is the reason our prayers for them have been answered:

> **Do not refuse a request to pray for the soul of another, even when you yourself lack the gift of prayer. For often the very faith of the person making the request will evoke the saving contrition of the one who is to offer the prayer.**

Do not become conceited when you have prayed for others and have been heard, for it is their faith which has been active and efficacious.

During our set times of prayer, we can often be distracted by thoughts—conversations we had, things we are anxious about, someone who has upset us, and so on. We should not allow these distractions to make us give up praying. We must persist; otherwise we will never learn to overcome such distractions and we will end up praying less and less. Those making a beginning of prayer frequently become distracted and have to make a conscious effort to bring their minds back to the task at hand. Those who are more experienced in the art of prayer are able to keep their minds focused. The true masters of prayer need not even make the effort to concentrate, but are enwrapped in the joy of God's presence and in the love of prayer:

The beginning of prayer is the expulsion of distractions from the very start by a single thought; the middle stage is the concentration on what is being said or thought; its conclusion is rapture in the Lord.

If you are careful to train your mind never to wander, it will stay by you even at mealtimes. But if you allow it to stray freely, then you will never have it beside you.

When we speak of distraction in prayer, we do not mean pausing to meditate on certain words of the prayers we are saying. If we are moved to tears or deeper contrition by a penitential prayer, or if we are overwhelmed by a sense of deep gratitude and wonder, we should not ignore this and just push on, even if it means we will not have time to complete our set prayers:

> **If it happens that, as you pray, some word evokes delight or remorse within you, linger over it; for at that moment our guardian angel is praying with us.**

It can be helpful, especially when we struggle to concentrate, to involve more than the mind in prayer. Rather than read our prayers silently, we can utter them aloud. This helps keep the mind focused. In addition to hearing the words of our prayer, we can involve the sense of smell by offering incense with our prayer. We can involve our sight (beyond the reading of words) by praying before an icon and a candle or vigil lamp. Thus prayer becomes not just something we say, but something we do. It becomes a physical action, a ritual of sorts.

In addition to involving our senses, it is helpful to involve physical action. Such actions could be:

- Making the sign of the cross
- Raising our hands
- Venerating (kissing) icons and the Bible
- Using a prayer rope to say the Jesus Prayer (repeating the invocation with each knot)
- Making prostrations (either full prostrations, which involve genuflections, or semi-prostrations, which are deep bows of reverence).

Thus our prayer is not passive but active, and it involves our whole being—body and soul. All of this can help us create a sense of purpose at our time of prayer, instead of it feeling like an obligation that we hastily squeeze into a free slot of time. In other words, it helps to have a particular place in the home that is set aside for prayer: a small table on which lies a prayer book, a Bible, an incense burner, a candle or vigil lamp; and on the wall above the table, icons of Christ, the Mother of God, and our patron saint. For families, it is helpful for parents and children to say a few simple prayers together at this prayer corner. The parents could continue with their own prayers together after putting the children to bed.

What about when we are not at home? When traveling, some find it helpful to have a small portable icon screen with them. When we are staying in hotels, we can set up that little icon screen, thus providing ourselves with a place of prayer wherever we go. Of course, prayer is no less prayer without icons and candles and incense, but these aids can help us when we feel spiritually dried up and do not feel like saying our prayers.

2. Mental Prayer

The second form of prayer is mental prayer, or prayer of the mind. This is when prayer goes from being something we do only at certain times of the day to being something we do inwardly throughout the day. Although it is thought of as the next level of prayer, it is something that even beginners can do. We can pray to God silently in our own words in almost any situation. But it takes time and experience in prayer to be able to learn the prayers of the Church by heart. The vast majority of Christians know the Lord's Prayer, but there are other prayers that Orthodox Christians should learn by heart, such as the Trisagion prayers ("Holy God, Holy Mighty One, Holy Immortal, have mercy on us . . .") and Psalm 50/51 ("Have mercy on me, O God . . ."), as well as the Symbol of Faith (the Nicene Creed).

Prayer of the mind should not replace prayer of the lips. If you are able to pray inwardly at various times throughout the day, it does not mean you should cease to say your prayers at set times (morning or evening, or both). As St. John writes: **Get ready for your set time of prayer by unceasing prayer in your soul.**

One prayer that is frequently encouraged in the practice of mental prayer is the Jesus Prayer. As we have said already, it is an invocation that can easily be repeated in any situation, and it is therefore ideal for continuous prayer throughout the day. As St. Paul says, "Pray without ceasing" (1 Thess. 5:17).

3. Prayer of the Heart

The highest level of prayer is prayer of the heart. This is when prayer is not only something we do, but something we are; when the Holy Spirit Himself prays within us. Perhaps this is what St. Paul meant when he said,

> "We do not know what we should pray for as we ought, but the Spirit Himself makes intercession for us with groanings which cannot be uttered." (Rom. 8:26)

> "It is no longer I who live, but Christ lives in me." (Gal. 2:20)

As with prayer of the mind, so too with prayer of the heart, the Jesus Prayer has enjoyed special attention as a method of acquiring such an elevated state of being. Unfortunately, many have come to see the practice of the Jesus Prayer as synonymous with prayer of the heart, but they are not one and the same thing. The Jesus Prayer is a means of acquiring perfect and ceaseless prayer; it is not the only means, but there can be little doubt that it is the most tried and tested method. But permit me to qualify the term *method*. While practitioners of the Jesus Prayer sometimes employ certain techniques (controlled breathing, certain postures, use of a prayer rope), prayer of the heart cannot be achieved simply by mastering any particular technique or method; nor can it be acquired by repetition and practice alone: it is truly a gift from God.

For this reason, I do not wish to say too much about it, as it is beyond my abilities to describe. What I will say is that even those very few who attain this level of prayer do not give up the practice of spoken and mental prayer. The former feed and nourish the latter, and vice versa. It is foolishness to expect to achieve pure prayer without ascetic struggle and virtue, without being purified of sin and mastering the passions; and it is equally foolish to think that prayer of the heart is a substitute for common worship.

When one attains prayer of the heart, everything becomes prayer, but the act of prayer remains a central part of Christian life no matter how holy we become:

> **However pure you may be, do not be forward in your dealings with God. Approach Him rather in all humility, and you will be given still more boldness. And even if you have climbed the whole ladder of the virtues, pray still for the forgiveness of sins. Heed Paul's cry regarding sinners "of whom I am first" (1 Tim. 1:15).**

Very few ever acquire prayer of the heart; very few truly *become* prayer. But we can all make prayer our way of life. If we silence our hearts and minds that we may listen to that "still small voice," we can all learn to pray "in Spirit and truth" (John 4:24). **Always be brave, and God will teach you your prayer.**

Step 29

Dispassion

Stars adorn the skies and dispassion has the virtues to make it beautiful. By dispassion I mean a heaven of the mind within the heart, which regards the artifice of demons as a contemptible joke. A man is truly dispassionate—and is known to be such—when he has cleansed the flesh of all corruption; when he has lifted his mind above everything created, and has made it master of all the senses; when he keeps his soul continually in the presence of the Lord and reaches out beyond the borderline of strength to Him. And there are some who would claim that dispassion is resurrection of the soul prior to that of the body, while others would insist that it is a perfect knowledge of God, a knowledge second only to that of the angels.

The highest level of virtue is the state of dispassion. By dispassion we do not mean an inability to experience the passions, but a complete mastery over them. The word *dispassionate* is sometimes misconstrued as *passionless.* Looking at the Greek word for dispassion does not often help dispel this misconception, for the word is *apatheia,* which sounds like apathy; but these two words have very different meanings. Dispassion is a state of being in which all the passions have been transformed into virtues:

> **A dispassionate soul is immersed in virtues as a passionate being is in pleasure.**

Until now I have tried to offer some advice and practical tips for how we can apply the *Ladder* to our lives and go about battling the passions and increasing the virtues. I cannot do this with dispassion, for no one can achieve it until he has acquired all the virtues, purified the senses, subjected the instincts to the will of the Spirit, and mastered the art of ceaseless prayer:

> **Just as a royal crown is not made up of one stone, so dispassion is incomplete if we neglect even one of the most ordinary virtues.**

To be dispassionate is **to sanctify the mind and to detach it from material things, and it does so in such a way that, after entering this heavenly harbor, a man, for most of his earthly life, is enraptured, like someone already in heaven, and he is lifted up to the contemplation of God.**

For most of us, our passions, sins, and desires distort the virtues. Our good intentions are mingled with ulterior motives, and our perception of God's will is clouded by our desires. This is why we often confuse our own will with the will of God. Only the dispassionate—those precious few!—are able really to know God's will, because for one who has achieved dispassion, **the will of the**

Lord becomes . . . a sort of inner voice through illumination. All human teaching is beneath him.

> When a man's senses are perfectly united to God, then what God has said is somehow mysteriously clarified. But where there is no union of this kind, then it is extremely difficult to speak about God. . . . The man who does not know God speaks about Him only in probabilities.

Theosis

Dispassion could perhaps be considered synonymous with another important word in Orthodox theology and spirituality: *deification*, or *theosis*, which means to attain the likeness of God, or, as countless Church Fathers have put it, "to become God by grace," that we "may be partakers of the divine nature" (2 Pet. 1:4).

I warned you that advanced spirituality can be complicated. Indeed, one cannot delve into advanced spirituality without getting deep into advanced theology, and the subject of dispassion and theosis is a case in point. I do not wish to simply overlook the subject, as it is so important to Orthodox mysticism and theology. So let us consider what we Orthodox mean by "becoming God."

The Orthodox doctrine of *theosis* is rooted in the Scriptures: "I said, 'You *are* gods, and all of you *are* children of the Most High'" (Ps. 81/82:6). But what does it mean for human beings to be gods? There is only one God, and He is God because He is eternal and uncreated. All other things were created by God from nothing (*ex nihilo*), which means that everything created is wholly contingent. So what does it mean for us who are "*but* dust and ashes" (Gen. 18:27) to "become" God?

It certainly does not mean that we evolve into the Deity—we cannot be what God is by nature (above being, eternal, all-knowing, all-powerful, all-holy, all-loving)—nor does it involve absorption into the Divine Being and a loss of our own personhood. Rather, it means to acquire the "likeness of God," which man was given the potential of achieving in Paradise (Gen 1:26) through synergy (the cooperation of the human will with divine grace). Deification is to become "holy, for I *am* holy" (Lev. 11:44), to become "perfect, just as your Father in heaven is perfect" (Matt. 5:48). And this has been made possible by the only human being who is God by nature: Jesus Christ. Because the Second Person of the Holy Trinity became what we are and shared in our humanity, we can become what He is and share in His divine glory.

But if no created being can become God—for He is "beyond all being" (in Greek, *hyperousios*)[47]—how do we explain this contradiction? The Orthodox Church explains it by a distinction between God's *essence* (what God is by nature) and His *energies* (what we can experience of God by His grace and condescension). God is by nature love, and by His grace we become love; He is by nature holy, and by His grace we are made holy; God is by nature eternal, and by His grace we have everlasting life. St. Maximus the Confessor explained it in the following way:

47 St. Romanos the Melodist, Kontakion of the Feast of the Nativity.

> A sure warrant for looking forward with hope to deification of human nature is provided by the incarnation of God, which makes man god to the same degree as God himself became man. . . . Let us become the image of the one whole God, bearing nothing earthly in ourselves, so that we may consort with God and become gods, receiving from God our existence as gods. For it is clear that He who became man without sin (cf. Heb. 4:15) will divinize human nature without changing it into the divine nature, and will raise it up for His own sake to the same degree as He lowered himself for man's sake. This is what St. Paul teaches mystically when he says, "that in the ages to come he might display the overflowing richness of His grace" (Eph. 2:7).[48]

Theosis, or dispassion, cannot be acquired with the intellect, but only by experience, meaning by synergy. We cannot be saved by faith alone, by grace alone, or by works alone. This principle lies at the heart of Orthodox mysticism. This is why prayer is so central to Christian spirituality. Theological study, the reading of the Scriptures, acts of charity—all these are good in themselves—but prayer is greater than all of them because it is a personal relationship with the Holy Trinity. The more pure and ceaseless our prayer, the more we grow in dispassion; the more we grow in dispassion, the closer we come to God; the closer we come to God, the more like Christ we become:

> **The dispassionate man no longer lives himself, but it is Christ Who lives in him (cf. Gal. 2:20).**

48 *Philokalia, op. cit.,* vol. 2, p. 178.

Dispassionate Love

If it is indeed true that "God is love" (1 John 4:8), then theosis, or union with God, is to acquire perfect love. So what, in the end, is the purpose of all this battling with passions and virtues, of this endless repentance and asceticism? The answer is divine love. The greater our dispassion, the greater our love:

> **To have dispassion is to have the fullness of love, by which I mean the complete indwelling of God in those who, through dispassion, are pure in heart for they shall see God (Matt. 5:8).**

Step 30

Faith, Hope, and Love

And now at last, after all that has been said, there remains that triad, faith, hope, and love, binding and securing the union of all. "But the greatest of these is love" (1 Cor. 13:13), since that is the very name of God Himself (cf. 1 John 4:8). To me they appear, one as a ray, one as light, and one as a disk,[49] and all as a single radiance and a single splendor.

We have finally reached the pinnacle of the Ladder, the summit of virtue, which is love. But from the above passage it is clear that just as Christians speak of God as Trinity, and should never think of Father, Son, and Holy Spirit in isolation from one another, so too when we speak of love, we cannot do so without including faith and hope. These three virtues—faith, hope, and love—are the "Holy Trinity" of the spiritual life. Without the former virtues, love becomes a vague sentiment, but when we see all three as one virtue, we are able to have a better grasp of what love means.

49 A common image among the Fathers to express the unity of the Holy Trinity.

God "desires all men to be saved and to come to the knowledge of the truth" (1 Tim. 2:4), and God said, "I am the truth": "I am the way, the truth, and the life" (John 14:6). So love, as a Christian virtue, or rather, *the* Christian virtue which **embraces all virtues**, is rooted in the knowledge of God. This is why Orthodox mysticism is never separated from dogma and theology. The purpose of both doctrine and mysticism is to know the true God, who is love:

> **Love, by its nature, is a resemblance to God, insofar as this is humanly possible. In its activity it is inebriation of the soul. Its distinctive character is to be a fountain of faith, an abyss of patience, a sea of humility.**

Only the dispassionate can acquire perfect faith, hope, and love, but we cannot even make a beginning of spiritual life if we do not possess these virtues to some degree. Thus this triad of virtues is not only the end and summit of the Ladder, but also its beginning:

> **A strong faith is the mother of renunciation. . . .**
> **Unswerving hope is the gateway to detachment. . . .**
> **Love of God is the foundation of exile.**

Faith

Many people do not understand why faith is a virtue, for faith is usually understood as nothing more than believing in something that cannot be proven. But when we speak of faith as a Christian virtue, we are speaking of something more specific than this. It is not a virtue to believe, for example, that what so-and-so told me is true or that the weather will be good tomorrow despite the gloomy forecast. Faith, or belief, does not mean gullibility. Unfortunately many think of religious faith in this way. But that kind of faith is far too rudimentary to deserve a place at the top of the ladder of Christian virtues. Faith as "the evidence of things not seen" (Heb. 11:1) is the beginning of faith, but not its end.

Faith, like hope and love, describes our relationship with God. The reason faith lies at the summit of the Ladder is that it both shapes our relationship with Him and, at the same time, is the fruit of that relationship. It is therefore better understood as trust, faithfulness, loyalty, and dedication. The more we come to know God, the more we trust in Him and the more we dedicate ourselves to Him. And yet, the greater our faith, the more we grow in the other virtues. We cannot begin to ascend the Ladder without faith, and yet the higher we ascend, the more faith increases.

Hope

If "faith is the substance of things hoped for" (Heb. 1:11), then it stands to reason that faith and hope go hand in hand. Some think of hope as wishful thinking or optimism, but not as a virtue. One may hope the weather will be good tomorrow just as one may stubbornly believe it will be. But as with faith, so too hope is the foundation and the fruit of our relationship with God. Our faith is one of hope in the Resurrection, in God's mercy, in the promise of His eternal Kingdom, of union with the Holy Trinity; and this hope is the source of divine love:

> **Hope is the power behind love. Hope is what causes us to look forward to the reward of love. Hope is an abundance of hidden treasures. It is the abundant assurance of the riches in store for us. It is . . . a doorway of love. It lifts despair and is the image of what is not yet present. When hope fails, so does love. Struggles are bound by it, labors depend on it, and mercy lies all around it.**

Those who continue to grow in dispassion ever increase in hope, for theosis does not have an end. The more we attain the likeness of God, the more we realize we have yet further to go, and so the greater the desire, the expectation, the hope that we will progress ever deeper into the infinite holiness of God. No one can go from the darkness into the dazzling light of divinity without being blinded by it. And so theosis is an eternal process of adjusting to a greater degree of divine light, love, holiness, and joy. It therefore stands to reason that hope does not end with salvation, with the fulfillment of God's everlasting Kingdom, but goes on and on, as our joy grows ever greater throughout eternity.

Love

St. Paul states that of the three virtues—faith, hope, and love—love is the greatest (1 Cor. 13:13). We said that prayer is the greatest activity of the spiritual life because it is by definition a relationship with God. Love is the same relationship but to an even greater and more intimate degree. This is why St. John says **love is greater than prayer.**

But we are told not only that love is the greatest virtue of all, but that "God is love" (1 John 4:8). Why is this so? Because God is Trinity: Father, Son, and Holy Spirit—three Persons in an eternal relationship of love, oneness, and unity. Love is relational and everlasting. Its fulfillment is a perfect harmony and union of persons. Thus the only one who truly is love by nature, who is love in His very essence, is God the Trinity.

The claim that "God is love" is unique to Christianity. Other monotheists believe that one God means one person—and there can be no true love without more than one person. Polytheists believe there are many distinct divine natures—and there can be no true love without a union of persons. God can be love only if He is Trinity, and therefore only Trinitarians can truly profess that "God is love."

Wounded by Love

The highest degree of love for God, which is the love of the dispassionate, is described in ways most of us would associate with passionate romance. This is not coincidental, for this is precisely how divine love is described by the great mystics of the Orthodox Church. The saints are sometimes described in Greek as *erastes* of God. *Erastes* is derived from the Greek word *eros,* so it quite literally means those who are "in love" with God.

Have you ever been so deeply and passionately in love with

someone that you are distracted by an obsession with that person? You may lose your appetite and forget to eat. You can think of nothing else. The object of your love is the last thing you think of when you go to bed, the first thing you think of when you wake up. The love can be so intense it even hurts. Now consider the following descriptions of the love of the dispassionate for God:

> Someone truly in love keeps before his mind's eye the face of the beloved and embraces it there tenderly. Even during sleep the longing continues unappeased, and he murmurs to his beloved. That is how it is for the body. And that is how it is for the spirit. A man wounded by love had this to say about himself—and it really amazes me—"I sleep (because nature demands it) but my heart is awake (because of the abundance of my love)" (Song of Songs 5:2).

> Holy love has a way of consuming some. This is what is meant by the one who said, "You have ravished our hearts, ravished them" (Song of Songs 4:9). And it makes others bright and overjoyed. In this regard it has been said: "My heart was full of trust and I was helped, and my flesh has revived" (Ps. 15:13), and a man flooded with the love of God reveals in his body, as if in a mirror, the splendor of his soul, a glory like that of Moses when he came face to face with God (cf. Exod. 34:29–35).

> Men who have attained this angelic state often forget to eat, and I really think they do not even miss their food. No wonder, since an opposite desire drives out the very wish to eat.

Lucky the man who loves and longs for God as a smitten lover does his beloved. . . . Lucky the man who is as passionately concerned with the virtues as a jealous husband watching over his wife.

We have heard St. John describe this relationship with God as being **wounded by love**. Love and beauty can bring a sensitive heart to tears, and yet they are tears not of regret or sorrow, but of joy—an almost painful joy. As Gandalf says at the end of *The Return of the King*, "I will not say, 'do not weep,' for not all tears are an evil." This being **wounded by love**, this deep compassion and sensitivity to the beauty of God and His creation, has been beautifully expressed by St. Isaac of Nineveh:

> What is a merciful heart? It is a heart, which is burning with love for the whole of creation: for human beings, for birds, for beasts, for demons—for all God's creatures. When such persons recall or regard these creatures, their eyes are filled with tears. An overwhelming compassion makes their heart grow small and weak, and they cannot endure to hear or see any kind of suffering, even the smallest pain, inflicted upon any creature. Therefore, these persons never cease to pray with tears even for the irrational animals, for the enemies of truth, as well as for those who do them evil, asking that these may be protected and receive God's mercy.[50]

Yet, while love can be "wounding," at the same time it makes everything seem bright and joyful. Thus divine love is the expulsion, or rather, the *transfiguration* of all the passions. The deeper

50 *Ascetic Treatises*, 48 (Wiesbaden, 1986), p. 30.

and more intense our love, the more cheerful and carefree we become. There is no place left for anger, malice, pride, gluttony, or selfishness:

> **If the sight of the one we love clearly makes us change completely, so that we turn cheerful, glad, and carefree, what will the face of the Lord Himself not do as He comes to dwell, invisibly, in a pure soul?**

The love described in the *Ladder* may give the impression that the dispassionate have their head in the clouds, that they are almost unaware of other people and disinterested in human affairs, but this would be a very one-sided understanding of the love St. John describes. For the love of God, however engrossing it may be, is never isolated from love for other people:

> **He who loves the Lord has first loved his brother, for the latter is proof of the former. Someone who loves his neighbor will never tolerate slanderers and will run from them as though from a fire. And the man who claims to love the Lord but is angry with his neighbor is like someone who dreams he is running.**

Love Has No End

We have described love and dispassion as the height of virtue, as the end of the Ladder and as spiritual perfection. These expressions require a significant qualification. While Christ told us that by imitating God's love, mercy, and forgiveness, we will "be perfect, just as your Father in heaven is perfect" (Matt. 5:48), we are speaking in a human language that cannot adequately convey the exact truth about God, who is beyond human understanding and all human speech. For God is infinitely perfect, and no matter how perfect we become, we will never enter into the essence of God; we will never become anywhere near as perfect as He is. That is why St. John describes dispassion as **an uncompleted perfection of the perfect.**

This applies even to the last step of the Ladder. If God is infinite, and if "God is love," then love is infinite, which means we will never reach the end of it. Even in the eternal life to come, we shall be forever increasing in love, forever plunging the infinite depths of God. Thus St. John describes love as **the progress of eternity:**

> **Love has no boundary, and both in the present and in the future age we will never cease to progress in it, as we add light to light.**

Each step of the Ladder can be understood as a progression in divine love, and with each step we come a little closer to the Trinity. Love is not only the final step of the Ladder, but every step of our divine ascent into the Kingdom of heaven, "the Alpha and the Omega, *the* Beginning and *the* End, the First and the Last" (Rev. 22:13).

Thus the *Ladder* concludes with the voice of God, who is love, inviting us to grow ever closer to Him, exhorting us to climb ever higher on the Ladder of Divine Love:

"So let this ladder teach you the spiritual union of the virtues. And I am there on the summit, for as the great man said, a man who knew me well: 'Remaining now are faith, hope, and love, these three. But love is the greatest of them all' (1 Cor. 13:13)."

About the Author

ARCHIMANDRITE Vassilios Papavassiliou is a priest of the Greek Orthodox Archdiocese of Thyateira and Great Britain. He was born in London in 1977 and holds degrees in pastoral and social theology, classics, and Byzantine music. He is the author of Ancient Faith Publishing's Meditation Series (*Meditations for Advent, Meditations for Great Lent, Meditations for Holy Week, Meditations for Pascha,* and *Meditations for the Twelve Great Feasts*) and is also the editor of *The Ancient Faith Prayer Book.*

An excerpt from

Archimandrite Vassilios Papavassiliou

Meditations for Holy Week

Dying and Rising with Christ

Introduction

HOLY WEEK, OR GREAT WEEK, is the heart of the Christian Orthodox Faith and the center of the yearly cycle of Orthodox feasts. Every year, our churches are packed at Holy Week, and come the last three days, they are bursting at the seams with both those who go to church every Sunday and those who attend only on special occasions. Holy Week brings the pious and the not-so-pious together in a way the most ambitious missionaries can only dream of. But Holy Week does not stand alone: It follows on from Great Lent, and the themes of the latter half of Great Lent are continued in the first half of Holy Week.

Holy Week begins with the first of three Matins services known as the Bridegroom Service. This service belongs to Great and Holy Monday but is usually celebrated on the evening of Palm Sunday. Each liturgical day of the Orthodox Church begins at sunset—the evening prior to the day in question. This practice of reckoning the evening as the beginning of the new day is an ancient Jewish tradition the Church has preserved in its system of worship. In the Creation narrative of Genesis, we read, "So the evening and the morning were the first day" (Gen. 1:5). Therefore, each Sunday begins with Vespers on Saturday evening, followed by Matins in the morning (in monasteries, it is held in the small hours of the morning).

However, in Holy Week, the usual pattern of holding Vespers in the evening and Matins in the morning is typically reversed. Thus in many parishes the evening services of Holy Week are Matins services, while the morning services are Vespers services.

One could divide Great and Holy Week into two halves. The first half (Great and Holy Monday–Wednesday) is dominated by the Bridegroom Service, which is based on the parable of the ten virgins (Matt. 25:1–13). The image of Christ as the Bridegroom of the Church reminds us of the intimate love and union between God and His people, and the absolute commitment and dedication to Christ that should define our relationship with Him. Many speak of the clergy as being "married to Christ" or "married to the Church," but the image of the Church as the "bride of Christ" reminds us that we are all married to Christ, and therefore complete dedication to Christ and His Church is not the vocation of a select few, but of every member of the Church.

In addition to the central image of the Bridegroom, the first three days of Holy Week are characterized by three key themes: repentance, vigilance, and the Second Coming. The parable of the ten virgins is, after all, a parable about the Last Judgment. It may seem curious that the Second Coming is a predominant theme, given that Holy Week is all about the First Coming: Christ coming to suffer and die for the world in order to give it new and everlasting life.

But the reason for this is fairly straightforward. The Crucifixion, death, and Resurrection of Christ inaugurated the last days. Thus our

Lord's final words on the Cross were, "It is finished" (John 19:30). The age of the Law has passed, and the age of Grace has begun. Through His Resurrection, the life of the age to come has already broken through.

No wonder the early Christians so eagerly anticipated the Lord's Second Coming and spoke of living in the last days. Ever since the Lord ascended to the heavenly Father, there has been nothing left for Christians to do but to carry out the commandments Christ gave us, repent of our sins, proclaim the Gospel to all people, and be ready for the Lord to come again. Yet even if the Second Coming is still very far off, the end is at hand for every one of us, since all of us will die. Therefore, the Church never ceases to exhort people of every age to be always ready to meet Christ.

The second half of Holy Week is the commemoration and celebration of our Lord's Passion, Crucifixion, death, burial, and Resurrection. And it is here that we are invited to enter the very essence of Orthodoxy. Holy Week is not simply a religious custom, but the heart of Christianity and the fundamental purpose of the Church in this world: to proclaim the good news that Christ has risen, offering us resurrection to eternal life.

Holy Week is a return to basics, a reintroduction to the very essence of Christian Orthodoxy. If anyone wishes to learn about the Orthodox Church, there is no better introduction than Holy Week. Here we will find the fundamental doctrines, practices, and ethos of our Church: theology, scripture, worship, prayer, asceticism, repentance, humility, compassion, love. All of this is to be found in abundance in the services of Holy Week, and Orthodox Christians never tire of rediscovering these fundamental beliefs year after year. This little book offers us a glimpse into the profound depth of these seven great and holy days of our Orthodox Church.

→ 1 ←

The Fruits of Repentance

Great and Holy Monday

On this day, like a saving light, the Holy Passion dawns on the world. For Christ in His goodness presses on to His sufferings. Though He holds all creation in the palm of His hand, yet He deigns to be hung on the Cross to save mankind. (First Kathisma of Great Monday Matins)

When the icon of Christ the Bridegroom is carried in procession to the center of the Church during the Matins service on the evening of Palm Sunday,[1] we sing:

Behold, the Bridegroom comes at midnight. And blessed is the servant whom He shall find watching. And again, unworthy is the servant whom He shall find heedless. Beware, therefore, O my soul: do not be weighed down with sleep, lest you be given up to death, and lest you be shut out of the Kingdom. But rouse yourself, crying, "Holy, holy, holy are You, our God." (Processional hymn, Great Monday Matins)

This hymn sums up the central themes of the first half of Holy Week:

1 Although parishes exist that celebrate Matins in the morning and Presanctified Liturgy in the evening, the opposite practice is so nearly universal that we will refer to it exclusively from here on.

vigilance and repentance. There is a sense of anticipation and urgency regarding Christ's coming to suffer and die for the world. The language of the Church here resembles its warning to be prepared for Christ's coming again. It is therefore no coincidence that the Gospel readings we hear at the Liturgy of the Presanctified Gifts[2] on Great Monday and Tuesday mornings are about the *Parousia* (the Second Coming). Throughout Holy Week, we are reminded that the Suffering Servant will come again as Judge, and so we are exhorted to repent that we may not be shut out of the "bridal chamber" of Christ (the Kingdom of Heaven):

> *Your bridal chamber I see adorned, my Savior, but I have no garment that I may enter. O Giver of Light, make radiant the vesture of my soul and save me. (Exaposteilarion of Great Monday Matins)*

The theme of preparing for Christ by bringing forth the fruit of repentance (Matt. 3:8) is conveyed in very certain terms through the Gospel theme of the cursing of the fig tree, which we hear at the Matins service for Great Monday:

> Now in the morning, as He returned to the city, He was hungry. And seeing a fig tree by the road, He came to it and found nothing on it but leaves, and said to it, "Let no fruit grow on you ever again." Immediately the fig tree withered away. (Matt. 21:18–19)

The exegesis of this seemingly bizarre action is given to us in the Church's hymns:

---

2 The Vesperal Liturgy of weekdays in Lent.

> *The fig tree is compared to the synagogue of the Jews, devoid of spiritual fruit, and Christ withers it with a curse. Let us flee a similar fate. (Synaxarion of Great Monday Matins)*

> *Mindful of what befell the fig tree, withered for its barrenness, O brethren, let us bear fruits worthy of repentance to Christ, who grants us His great mercy. (Aposticha of Great Monday Matins)*

But what are these fruits of repentance? To answer this, let us return to the main hymn of the Bridegroom service (*Behold, the Bridegroom comes at midnight*). This hymn, as we have said, is based on the parable of the ten virgins, which we hear on Great Tuesday morning:

> "Then the kingdom of heaven shall be likened to ten virgins who took their lamps and went out to meet the bridegroom. Now five of them were wise, and five *were* foolish. Those who *were* foolish took their lamps and took no oil with them, but the wise took oil in their vessels with their lamps. But while the bridegroom was delayed, they all slumbered and slept. And at midnight a cry was *heard:* 'Behold, the bridegroom is coming; go out to meet him!' Then all those virgins arose and trimmed their lamps. And the foolish said to the wise, 'Give us *some* of your oil, for our lamps are going out.' But the wise answered, saying, '*No,* lest there should not be enough for us and you; but go rather to those who sell, and buy for yourselves.' And while they went to buy, the bridegroom came, and those who were ready went in with him to the wedding; and the door was shut. Afterward the other virgins came also, saying, 'Lord, Lord, open to us!' But he answered and said, 'Assuredly, I say to you, I do not know you.' Watch therefore, for you know neither the day nor the hour in which the Son of Man is coming." (Matt. 25:1–13)

The parable illustrates the typical custom of marriage among the people of Israel at that time. After the engagement ceremony, the bridegroom, accompanied by relatives and friends, would make his way to the bride's home, where she would await him in her best attire, surrounded by friends. The wedding ceremony would usually take place at night; therefore, the friends of the bride would meet the bridegroom with lit lamps. Since the exact time of the bridegroom's arrival would not be known, those who were waiting would provide themselves with oil in case it should burn out in the lamps. The bride, with her face covered by a veil, together with the bridegroom and all the participants in the ceremony, would make their way to the bridegroom's house, singing and dancing. The doors would be shut, the marriage contract signed, blessings would be pronounced in honor of the couple, the bride would uncover her face, and the marriage feast would begin.

The parable makes it clear that the foolish virgins had not made the necessary preparation for the bridegroom's coming, and this lack of preparation is conveyed in their lack of oil. The oil represents the virtues, and particularly the virtues of mercy and compassion.

It is telling that some of our Church Fathers and hymn writers, who were great lovers of word play, make a comparison between the Greek word for oil, *elaion,* and the Greek word for mercy, *eleos.* And mercy is what the Church recognizes the oil to symbolize in this parable. This is why the foolish virgins cannot take the oil from the wise. Mercy and compassion are virtues we must acquire and labor for. There is no easy or lazy solution. We must bring forth the "fruits of repentance," that is to say, the works that flow from a genuine contrition and conversion, from dedicated vigilance and sincere faith:

> *Brethren, let us greet the Bridegroom with love, trimming our lamps so that we reflect virtue and true faith. So shall we be ready, like the prudent maidens of the Lord, to enter with Him into the wedding feast. For being God, the Bridegroom bestows on all the gift of an incorruptible crown. (Kathisma, Matins of Great Tuesday)*

> *I have succumbed to spiritual indolence, O Christ my Bridegroom, and hold no lamp alight with virtue. I am like the foolish virgins, wandering about when it was time to act. Master, do not seal against me the wellsprings of Your pity; but rouse me to shake off the gloom of sleep and lead me with the prudent maids into Your bridal chamber. Here the clear song of those who rejoice can be heard, singing, "O Lord, glory to You!" (The Praises, Matins of Great Tuesday)*

The fruits of repentance are above all acts of mercy and compassion, works of humility and love. If we pay careful attention to the hymns, themes, and biblical readings of Holy Week, we will notice that the themes of oil and repentance, humility and love, emerge time and again in the Church's services. The foolish virgins' lack of the "oil of mercy" in the parable of the bridegroom vividly reminds us of our Lord's exhortation: "Go and learn what *this* means: 'I desire mercy and not sacrifice'" (Matt. 9:13; see also Hos. 6:6).

To be prepared for the Lord's coming, it is not enough to "discern the signs of the times" (Matt. 16:3); there must be a change from within, a conversion to humility, divine love, and mercy. Thus on Great Monday, the Church brings us back to the central theme of the Gospel reading for the fifth Sunday of Lent (Mark 10:32–45), and we are reminded of our Lord's commandment to imitate Him by being humble and loving one another:

> *"All will know you are My disciples if you keep My commandments," said the Lord as He approached His Passion. "Be at peace with yourselves and with everyone; and in your humility you will be exalted. Confessing Me as Lord, sing praise and exaltation forever.*
>
> *"Let your ways be contrary to those of the Gentiles and their lords. That is not My inheritance to you; a selfish will is tyranny. So he who would be first among you, let him be the last. Confessing Me as Lord, sing praise and exaltation forever." (Eighth Ode of the Canon of Great Monday Matins)*

> *In Your perfect wisdom, You counseled Your disciples: "Casting off every impure impulse, acquire a prudent mind worthy of the divine Kingdom. Thus shall you be glorified, shining more brightly than the sun."*
>
> *"Consider Me," You said to Your disciples, Lord, "and do not harbor proud thoughts, but keep company with the meek. The cup that I drink you will drink, and so you will be glorified with Me in the Kingdom of the Father." (Magnificat of Great Monday Matins)*

How are we to acquire such an incredible degree of love, compassion, and humility? The answer is given to us in the following hymn:

> *As the Lord was going to His voluntary Passion, He said to the Apostles on the way, "Behold, we go up to Jerusalem, and the Son of Man will be delivered up as it is written of Him." Come, therefore, let us also go with Him, purified in mind. Let us be crucified with Him and die with Him to the pleasures of this life. Then we shall live with Him and hear Him say, "I go no more to the earthly Jerusalem to suffer, but to*

My Father and your Father; to My God and your God. And I will raise you up to the Jerusalem on high, to the kingdom of heaven." (Praises of Great Monday Matins)

If we are not willing to endure hardship for God and neighbor, if we refuse to practice asceticism, we will always be too weak and selfish to practice perfect and selfless love. True love and compassion mean self-denial.

Many people are perfectly willing to deny themselves certain things and make sacrifices for some greater purpose. An athlete endures physical hardship and observes strict diets in order to reach and maintain the physical condition required to succeed in his sport. Others abstain from certain foods for reasons of health or beauty. Yet tell such people to do the same for Christ and one is often met with a whole host of objections, with jeering or even anger.

To be Christians means to take up Christ's Cross and follow Him to Golgotha. In other words, we are called to voluntarily sacrifice the pleasures of this life that we may reach and maintain the required spiritual condition to practice self-denying love. We are invited to journey with our Lord to His Passion and death by dying to the self, for it is only by choosing to die with Christ—that is to say, by sacrificing the pleasures of the flesh and the stubbornness of pride and selfishness—that we can rise with Him to the new, transfigured, and everlasting life of the Resurrection.

Other Books by Archimandrite Vassilios Papavassiliou

Meditations for Great Lent

Reflections on the Triodion

The Lenten Triodion exhorts us, "Let us observe a fast acceptable and pleasing to the Lord." Using hymns from the Triodion and the Scripture readings appointed for the season, *Meditations for Great Lent* shows us how to make our fast acceptable: to fast not only from food but from sin; to fast with love and humility, as a means to an end and not an end in itself. Keep this gem of a book with you to inspire you for the Fast and to dip into for encouragement as you pursue your Lenten journey.

Meditations for Holy Week

Dying and Rising with Christ

Archimandrite Vassilios brings his liturgical and devotional insights and warm, accessible style to bear on the services of Holy Week, helping the reader enter fully into this most rich and intense period of the Christian year.

Meditations for Pascha

Reflections on the Pentecostarion

Far from being merely a "vacation from fasting," the Pascha season is a time that, properly understood, can greatly enrich our faith. During the Pascha season, we celebrate and rejoice in our Lord's Resurrection and we prepare for the great feast of the Holy Spirit descending upon us.

Meditations for Advent

Preparing for Christ's Birth

by Archimandrite Vassilios Papavassiliou

The author of the popular *Meditations for Great Lent* takes us through the hymnography, Scripture readings, and iconography for the forty days leading up to the Nativity of Christ, showing how a full understanding of the Incarnation can enrich our spiritual lives.

Meditations for the Twelve Great Feasts

Becoming Fully Human in Christ

This volume completes the popular Meditations series by taking a brief look at each of the major feasts of the church year. Fr. Vassilios brings out the gems embodied in the church's hymnography to enhance our understanding and participation in these milestones of our salvation.

The Ancient Faith Prayer Book

Edited by Archimandrite Vassilios Papavassiliou, the *Ancient Faith Prayer Book* brings together the most ancient and popular prayers of Orthodox Christians with some additions that address issues of contemporary life, all rendered in elegant contemporary English and presented in a compact format (4-1/2 X 7 inches) for ease of use.

Other Books of Interest

Pilgrimage to Pascha

A Daily Devotional for Great Lent

by Archpriest Steven John Belonick

Second edition edited by Deborah Malacky Belonick

This unpretentious little book of meditations based on Scripture, ancient hymns, and writings from Church Fathers will nourish the souls of reflective seekers during the forty-day period of Great Lent. Authors of each meditation have delved deeply into the sins and shortcomings of their own hearts, enabling readers to share in a collective human experience - from darkness to light, from despair to hope, and from isolation to commonality in the body of Christ - as they move steadily toward our Lord's Resurrection.

Toolkit for Spiritual Growth

A Practical Guide to Prayer, Fasting, and Almsgiving

by Fr. Evan Armatas

Are you a new Orthodox Christian, confused about what you need to do to grow in your Faith? Or perhaps you've been Orthodox for some time but could use a refresher course in basic spirituality. Popular podcaster Fr. Evan

Armatas explains the fundamentals of the three-legged stool of Orthodox practice - prayer, almsgiving, and fasting - in terms that everyone can understand and implement. Let Fr. Evan help you establish your life in Christ on a firm footing.

Bread & Water, Wine & Oil

by Archimandrite Meletios Webber

According to two thousand years of experience, Orthodoxy shows us how to be transformed by the renewing of our mind—a process that is aided by participation in the traditional ascetic practices and Mysteries of the Church. In this unique and accessible book, Archimandrite Meletios Webber first explores the role of mystery in the Christian life, then walks the reader through the seven major Mysteries of the Orthodox Church, showing the way to a richer, fuller life in Christ.

The Scent of Holiness

by Constantina Palmer

Every monastery exudes the scent of holiness, but women's monasteries have their own special flavor. Join Constantina Palmer as she makes frequent pilgrimages to a women's monastery in Greece and absorbs the nuns' particular approach to their spiritual life. If you're a woman who's read of Mount Athos and longed to partake of its grace-filled atmosphere, this book is for you. Men will find it a fascinating read as well.

A Book of Hours

by Patricia Colling Egan

Eastern and Western Christians share a rich spiritual heritage in the Hours of Prayer—the brief services of praise and psalmody that mark the progress of each day, sanctifying the hours of our lives. In this gem of a book, Patricia Egan digs deeply into the meaning of each of the Hours, drawing on poetry, nature, experience, and theology to show how the services reflect the different aspects of our salvation and our lives. *A Book of Hours* is an excellent companion for anyone who wants to experience the blessing of praying through the Hours of each day.

All titles available at store.ancientfaith.com. Most also available as ebooks.

Ancient Faith Publishing hopes you have enjoyed and benefited from this book. The proceeds from the sales of our books only partially cover the costs of operating our nonprofit ministry—which includes both the work of **Ancient Faith Publishing** and the work of **Ancient Faith Radio.** Your financial support makes it possible to continue this ministry both in print and online. Donations are tax-deductible and can be made at www.ancientfaith.com.

To view our other publications,
please visit our website: **store.ancientfaith.com**

Bringing you Orthodox Christian music, readings, prayers, teaching, and podcasts 24 hours a day since 2004 at **www.ancientfaith.com**